A Gift of Music

Great Composers and Their Influence

*Jane Stuart Smith
and Betty Carlson*

with a Preface by Francis A. Schaeffer

CROSSWAY BOOKS ● WESTCHESTER, ILLINOIS
A DIVISION OF GOOD NEWS PUBLISHERS

Cover photo: "The Month of May" from
Les Très Riches Heures du Duc de Berry
by the Limbourg brothers, 1416 A.D.
Used by permission of the
Musée Condé à Chantilly, France.

PRINTING HISTORY
Good News Publishers cloth edition published 1978
Crossway Books third printing 1980
Excerpts appeared in Eternity
Crossway Books paperback edition / May 1983

Printed in the United States of America

Library of Congress Catalog Card Number 83-70798
ISBN 0-89107-293-4

This book is dedicated with deep appreciation to June Samson who first introduced me to great music.

Contents

Preface

There are things in the Christian world which cause us to be sad. One of these is that for many Christians classical music is a complete vacuum. This robs individual Christians and their children of one of the very rich areas of joy in this world. Incidentally, an ignorance of classical music also separates us from many people to whom we wish to speak, and thus is a hindrance in our communication with them. But the central sadness of knowing little about classical music consists in the loss the Christian experiences in one of the areas of the affirmation of life.

In this book there is a wealth of detail concerning classical music which many Christians will not have thought about at all, and those who do know something of classical music will certainly find added detail which will further enrich their enjoyment of it. I really do hope that this book stimulates interest in classical music among many Christians. One does not need to be an expert to begin to have an enjoyment of such music. I remember what opened the door to classical music for me when I was young—suddenly hearing the *1812 Overture*. Though it would be far from my favorite now, the dynamic force of it grasped me, and from that time on I went from composer to composer with a growing interest. It has been one of the rich things in my own life.

Of course, tastes differ and many interested in classical music might have chosen different composers to deal with in the book and different selections by those composers. As in all discussions in the area of art there will also be differences concerning some of the conclusions. This is inevitable in any area in art and may perhaps be especially true in music. On the other hand, I think there will be no one who will not find stimulating insights and fresh details.

Betty Carlson came to us while we lived in Champéry, and she became a Christian in Chalet Bijou there. Later she bought Chalet Chesalet in Huémoz, and has been very much a part of the community ever since. She is a worker in L'Abri.

Jane Stuart Smith was singing opera and studying in Milan when she first visited us after L'Abri began in Huémoz. She became a Christian here and was instrumental in opening the first door for us to work among the musicians in Milan, and then eventually to the beginning of a Bible study class there. Later she became a worker in L'Abri and then later still a member of L'Abri, which she still is.

Chalet Chesalet has been a real shelter to many hundreds of people who have stayed at L'Abri through the years. There are people all over the world who now understand something of classical music and have a deep enjoyment of it because of their times at Chalet Chesalet. They have profited from the discussions about music and from listening to the large library of recorded classical music available in Chalet Chesalet. Jane Stuart Smith has added a very special musical contribution to L'Abri, and we now look for this book to open the doors to a new affirmation of life in the area of music for many Christians.

—Frances A. Schaeffer

Prelude

When considering composers who are among the greatest in Western history, the more important question is not, "What do we think of Handel (or Mozart, or Stravinsky)," but "What would Handel think of us?" I believe Handel would be surprised that we only listen to some of his music, like *Messiah* and *The Water Music Suite*, when he wrote so many other magnificent compositions. And in listening to the elegant, carefree sounds of Mozart it is only fair that we remember he scarcely ever received just payment for his works and was buried at an early age in a pauper's grave. Stravinsky might want us to keep in mind that yes, his music is at times "lean," but he was trying to strip away the heaviness of sound left over from the 19th century.

Most of all, the purpose of this book is to encourage listening to the finest music with understanding and pleasure, and to stretch one's ears and imagination. The more we acquaint ourselves with that which is truly great and beautiful, the more we will dislike and turn away from that which is shallow and ugly. Also we want to show that what each artist believes in his heart and mind effects his creativity and those who follow him.

Concerning certain limitations in the following chapters: This is not a history of music, nor is it a book only on Christian composers. Obviously, there is no attempt to discuss all types of music (that would require several volumes). We have chosen to restrict our choice of composers to the area of art music, or classical music as it is also called. For the sake of brevity some of your favorite composers (and ours) have been omitted. We are aware that one cannot avoid reflecting subjective judgment and personal taste, but we have attempted to present the historical facts accurately, and to speak of the weaknesses and foibles of "our" composers with compassion, recognizing that no one is perfect.

The following chapters have been selected from Farel House lectures given by Jane Stuart Smith at L'Abri Fellowship in Switzerland. Miss Smith, a former opera singer and ardent student of music, art, and literature, is asked at the conclusion of each lecture, by an eager group of students, professors, musicians, and other listeners, for "further information." This book is a response to these many inquiries.

Jane Stuart Smith has gathered the material for her lectures over the years from a variety of books and encyclopedias, a file of clippings and notes, and through an active musical life in various countries. I hope the reader has the same excitement in learning that has been my experience while shaping the rather sketchy lecture notes into book form.

In particular we are indebted to Donald Jay Grout for his outstanding book, *A History of Western Music.* Also we give special thanks to Shirley Henn, Mildred Mitchell, and Thelma Diercks for their help in our research in the Hollins College library. We are grateful for the encouragement given by Liggie Smith, our friends in Switzerland, who have carried on our work while we were away to write the book, and in particular, Rosemary Sperry, who has taken care of Chalet Chesalet, the chickens, and Owl in our absence.

—Betty Carlson

"A man that has a taste of music, painting, or architecture, is like one that has another sense, when compared with such as have no relish of those arts."

—Joseph Addison

Introduction
Psalms in Western Music History

"Sing unto the Lord with the harp; with the harp, and the voice of a psalm. With trumpets and sound of cornet make a joyful noise before the Lord, the King." Psalm 98:5, 6

Do you know that Psalm 98 inspired Isaac Watts to write "Joy to the World"? That Martin Luther's great Reformation hymn, "A Mighty Fortress," is a paraphrase of Psalm 46? That the often-sung "Doxology" dates back to Calvin's 16th Century Genevan Psalter?

"Psalms are sweet for every age and they create a bond of unity when the whole people raise their voice in one choir," said Ambrose, Bishop of Milan, in the fourth century.

This most wonderful of all hymn books has been cherished by God's people in every age. The Book of Psalms has been the single most productive source of texts for musical compositions in Western music. Psalm singing is the earliest recorded musical activity of the church,

15

perhaps in response to the Apostle Paul's admonition to "be filled with the Spirit, speaking to yourselves in psalms and hymns and spiritual songs, singing and making melody in your heart to the Lord" (Eph. 5:18-19). The very backbone of sacred music has been the Psalms.

Psalms have been in the center of worship just as we find them in the middle of the Bible. The Psalter is an anthology of poems written by various authors over a period of about 1,000 years, but David probably wrote more than half of the 150 Psalms.

Psalms were central in Christ's devotion and worship. He often quoted from them and verified that they were referring to Him, as in Luke 24:44: ". . . all things must be fulfilled, which were written in the law of Moses, and in the prophets, and in the psalms concerning me." Before going to the Garden of Gethsemane and later to his crucifixion, Christ sang Psalms with his disciples.

Paul and Silas sang hymns of praise to God in the Philippian jail. Throughout the Middle Ages the walls of European monasteries echoed with the chanting of Psalms, and the great Reformers planted the Psalter in the heart of their service. Even today Psalms are read more widely than any poetry, and are used regularly in all Christian churches and Jewish synagogues.

Trust in the Living God who hears prayer and answers is the basic theme throughout the Psalms. In the Psalms God is a Person who acts in nature and history, and in the lives of men and women. He is a God of mercy and truth, full of compassion for suffering human beings. Psalms were not written as cold liturgy, but as personal expressions in relation to the Sovereign God of the universe who cares for those who trust Him. Human emotions are dealt with in a personal way. John Calvin said that he saw himself in the Psalms and applied them to his own situation.

The key word of the Psalms is worship, and this is heightened by musical settings. Poetry is the form of expression most appropriate to describe feelings, and with music added the emotional intensity is increased. The word "Psalm" comes from the Greek word *psalmoi* meaning "twangings of harp strings" which reminds us that Psalms are to be sung.

The history of music until A.D. 200 is shrouded in darkness because of the problem of notation. We have none of the original music that Psalms were set to, although we know that Hebrew music was mainly vocal with much use of antiphonal singing and some instrumental accompaniment.

Because composers use Psalms as texts for musical compositions does not necessarily mean that they believe the content. One must examine a person's life as well as what he professes to believe. Even then there are mysteries that belong only to God. However, we can ask: Why have great composers used Psalms as a source of texts more often than any other book? Why are the Psalms so important— even to the non-Christian? One obviously knows objectively that they are great literature, but we sense there is something more. Yes, there is the honesty of the Psalms, the melody and beauty, but more important is the truth that the Psalms are the inspired word of the Living God.

As we follow the flow of music history we can start with Ambrose, Bishop of Milan (339-397), who emphasized a true biblical Christianity. Ambrose introduced antiphonal psalmody and hymns to the west, and the Ambrosian Chant is still sung in Milan today. Augustine (354-430) became a Christian through the powerful preaching of Ambrose. Augustine later said that hymns are praises to God with singing. According to tradition, as Ambrose baptized Augustine, the two improvised the "Te Deum Laudamus" ("We Praise Thee, O God") in alternate verses. This may well be true since it was the practice of the early church to create hymns when inspired by strong religious feeling. The "Te Deum" is believed to have been written about that time (late fourth century) and is one of the few prose texts composed then.

Pope Gregory I (reigned 590-604) brought many musical reforms into the church. He was responsible for having all the modes of the Western church arranged into a systematic whole. In his honor this music is called the Gregorian Chant. All musical instruments were restricted, and only men were allowed to sing the Gregorian Chant in the services. This music, with its impersonal mystical quality is a powerful expression of Romanesque art. It is startling to realize that three-fourths of the Gregorian Chants are made up of either entire Psalm texts or selected verses. These Chants were the source and inspiration of a large proportion of all sacred Western music up to the sixteenth century. As they are one of the great treasures of Western civilization, it illustrates again the importance of Psalms in music history. Throughout the Renaissance the Psalm settings of Andrea and Giovanni Gabrieli and Sweelinck continued to inspire great music.

Martin Luther (1483-1546) included music as a vital part of worship in the form of congregational chorale singing (with all voices included). This practice helped to sow the seeds of a musical renaissance in the German-speaking lands. The chorale was an effective representation of Scripture. Luther, described as an accomplished amateur, wrote a number of chorales. His best known, "A Mighty Fortress is our God," helped to spread the Reformation through Europe. Luther called the Psalter "A Bible in Miniature," and it was his constant companion. It is said that whenever he heard discouraging news he would say to his family or friends, "Come, let us sing the 46th Psalm." Luther undoubtedly inspired others to write chorales or to sing them when he said, "He who despises music, as do all the fanatics, does not please me. Music is a gift of God, not a gift of men. . . . After theology I accord to music the highest place and greatest honour."

As John Calvin (1509-1564) prohibited the singing of texts not found in the Bible, the only notable productions of the Calvinist churches were the various translations of the Book of Psalms set to music. Elaborate music was prohibited, so the Genevan Psalter is compiled of simple four-part settings which are excellent for devotional music. In his preface to the Genevan Psalter of 1542 Calvin connects religious music with prayer: "As for public prayers, there are two kinds: the ones with words alone, the others with singing."

The principal French Psalter was published in 1562 with music composed by Louis Bourgeois, which includes our often-sung "Doxology." The French Huguenots sang Psalms in court and camp. It has been said that the Protestant Reformation exercised a greater influence upon the historical course of religious music specifically, and European music generally, than any other movement initiated in the Renaissance.

Heinrich Schütz (1585-1672), the greatest German composer of the middle 17th century, was one of the most important musical figures of the Baroque period which culminated in the towering works of Bach and Handel. Schütz wrote his music in a clear, careful style so that people would get the message of the words. His desire was to proclaim biblical truth. His settings of Psalms to music throughout his long, creative life are the heart of his work.

Johann Sebastian Bach (1685-1750) is considered by many Christians and secular critics to be the greatest composer of all time. Bach spent his life in musical service to God. He wrote some of the greatest devotional music the world has ever known. The core of his creative work is a vast treasure of cantatas which make up more than half of his music. These are often based on Psalms. Cantata 131, for example, is a setting of the moving penitential Psalm 130.

Unlike many intellectuals of today, who know little or

nothing about the Bible, educated persons of the 18th century were acquainted with Scripture. George Frideric Handel (1685-1759), "The Prince of Music," was thoroughly familiar with the Bible, and he delighted in the Psalms. He used them in such monumental oratorios as *Messiah* and *Israel in Egypt.* The antiphonal singing we hear in his settings of Psalms 110 and 113 has roots in Jewish worship. His Chandos Anthems with Psalm texts brought Anglican music of the Baroque period to its culmination.

Franz Joseph Haydn (1732-1809) was a God-fearing man. He wrote his masterpiece *The Creation* in the later years of his life, having been inspired by Handel's *Messiah.* One of the supreme moments in the oratorio is "The Heavens Are Telling," Haydn's setting of verses from Psalm 19. His friend, Wolfgang Amadeus Mozart (1756-1791), perhaps the most purely musical composer, did a magnificent arrangement of the shortest of all Psalms, the praise-filled 117th Psalm.

Ludwig van Beethoven (1770-1827), at one time the rebellious pupil of Haydn, was the great revolutionary composer whose music was the bridge from the Classical period to Romanticism. In his setting of verses from Psalm 19, "The Heavens Are Telling," one can almost see the stars shining.

These composers will be discussed in more detail in subsequent chapters; I am mentioning only a few here to show how in all periods of history the Psalms have acted as the "salt of the earth" in music. Countless composers have not been included. To do justice to this theme, one would need to write volumes. What riches have come from the Psalms right down into the last half of the 20th century!

The early Romantic Jewish-Christian composer, Felix Mendelssohn (1809-1849), set many Psalms. One example is his great oratorio, *Elijah,* which contains "Lift Thine Eyes to the Mountains" from Psalm 121.

The German Classic-Romantic composer, Johannes

Brahms (1833-1897), said that he could find his Bible in the darkest night, because he kept it always with him. The music of Brahms, like that of Schütz and Bach, is inspired by a deep concern with man's mortal lot and his hope of heaven. From his beautiful *German Requiem* there is a setting of Psalm 84. As one hears the different languages to these Psalm settings, one is aware of their international influence.

Arthur Honegger (1892-1955), one of "Les Six" (a group of French composers), became famous after his oratorio *King David* was performed in a barnlike theatre at Mezières near Lausanne, Switzerland. The text contains many Psalms and has as its theme, "Be not afraid: Put your trust in God."

A distinguished piece of the 20th century is Stravinsky's *Symphony of Psalms.* Stravinsky was one of the prime shapers of contemporary music in this century.

After introducing to the 20th century a theory which is known as the "12-tone row" or "serial technique," Arnold Schönberg (1874-1951) at the end of his life seemed unable to live with it himself. His last completed work was the choral setting of Psalm 130, "Out of the depths have I cried unto Thee, O Lord." He dedicated it to the Israeli nation.

Krzysztof Penderecki (1933-   ) born in Poland, is one of the outstanding composers of our time. His first published work was *Psalms of David.*

The vast treasure of Christian hymnology has its wellspring in the Book of Psalms. The grand note of the great hymns is praise to God through His Word. The father of English hymnody, Isaac Watts, wrote many paraphrases of the Psalms including "O God, Our Help in Ages Past," a paraphrase of Psalm 90, as well as "Joy to the World," based on Psalm 98. Even today Psalms contribute to our hymns.

Countless others have set Psalms to music. Among the

best known are Johann Walther, Praetorius, Buxtehude, Vivaldi, Marcello, Schubert, Dvorak, Liszt, Bruckner, Distler, and Americans William Billings, Charles Ives, and Paul Creston. It is interesting to note that the first book known to have been both written and printed in the English colonies of America was the *Bay Psalm Book.*

It is the prayer of those of us who live and work at L'Abri Fellowship that we turn continually to the Bible for knowledge and wisdom, not only to learn how to live with hope in a fallen world, but to receive inspiration to be more creative. To the Christian musician in particular, I urge you to live in the midst of the Psalms, singing them and writing your own music to the glory of God.

Recommended Reading
King James Version of the Bible

Meyer, F.B., *Gems From the Psalms.* Westchester, Illinois: Good News Publishers, 1976.

Scroggie, W. Graham. *Psalms.* London: Pickering and Inglis Ltd., 1965.

Recommended Listening
Gregorian Chant (Solesmes Recordings)
"A Mighty Fortress is Our God"
Schütz: Psalm 121
Handel: Chandos Anthems
      Dixit Dominus
Bach: Cantata 131
Haydn: "The Heavens are Telling" *(The Creation)*
Mozart: Psalm 117 (Laudate Dominum)
Beethoven: "The Heavens are Telling"
Mendelssohn: "Lift Thine Eyes to the Mountains" *(Elijah)*
Brahms: "How Lovely are Thy Dwellings" *(German Requiem)*

Honegger: "Be Not Afraid" *(King David)*
Stravinsky: *Symphony of Psalms*
Penderecki: *Psalms of David*
"Our God, Our Help in Ages Past" (words: Isaac Watts)
Ives: *Psalms*

Chapter I
Heinrich Schütz
(1585-1672)

"Thy statutes have been my songs in the house of my pilgrimage." Psalm 119:54

Imagine two choirs, six soloists, two violins and an organ combining to present the account of Paul's conversion. First, from one side of the chancel you hear the deep-toned solo basses asking, "Saul, Saul, Why persecutist thou me?" Soon the tenor, alto and soprano soloists join in the questioning. The rhythm is accelerated, interrupted by cadences. The choirs answer the calls, increasing the volume to a *fortissimo* climax, finally subsiding to an echo effect by the sopranos.

Are you hearing a supernatural invocation?

No, it is one of the impressive works of Heinrich Schütz whose name is hardly a household word. This German law student-turned-composer studied music in Italy where the Baroque sound fired his imagination. He returned home to apply Italian methods of word-painting to German texts. He developed the free-style setting of Scriptural texts and emerged one of the creative genuises in musical history.

Too often we don't realize how much someone in the past has influenced what we enjoy today. Schütz's many pupils helped spread his influence—even to Bach who studied under one of them. Had Schönberg or Cage preceded Bach instead of Schütz, we might not have had Bach—now considered to be among the world's greatest composers and master of the church cantata.

We must be careful not to forget history or the roots of our culture. In cultivating the old, one has a better understanding of the new. Much of what we hear today is dross, but having said that we cannot dismiss all modern music. We need to be sufficiently informed to understand why it is the way it is. And, we must remember that the test of time is often necessary. Great music lives on. Heinrich Schütz is one whose music has survived.

Schütz is considered the greatest German composer of the middle 17th century and is one of the most important musical figures of the early Baroque period. He became famous in his lifetime, yet he had a lonely life filled with hardship and affliction, due partly to the upheaval of war. In addition to the musical heritage he gave us, Schütz has something to say to us through the example of his life.

It began in 1585. Schütz was born into a world of Shakespeare and Cervantes, and also one of religious strife climaxed in the Thirty Years War. Like such outstanding composers as Bach, Haydn, and Schubert, he owed the start of his career to a fine treble voice. He began to study law, but a nobleman who recognized Schütz's abilities and eagerness for knowledge sent him to Venice to study music in 1609.

Venice, "The Queen of the Adriatic," with its lagoons, warm light, and luminous colors is unique in the world. It was built on 118 miniature islands separated by 160 canals which are its streets. The islands are connected by 400 bridges. In the time of Schütz, Venice was a spiritual capital of the art and music world. The fascination of light, water, and air is still hypnotic. Quiet, mysterious reflections stir the senses, and gondolas still decorate the canals.

When Heinrich Schütz arrived in Venice he was received with great kindness by Giovanni Gabrieli (1555-1612), the most renowned Venetian composer of the time. Schütz, who was a gentle, humble individual with a desire to learn, was invited to stay in the home of the composer. A rich friendship developed between the teacher and the pupil, and for four years Schütz was instructed by the great Gabrieli in the "grand Italian style." It became the principal foundation upon which German composers were to build their music.

Gabrieli has been called the "musical Titian" of Venice. His music is brilliant and powerful and few composers have ever achieved such splendor and grandeur in musical tones. In fact, Gabrieli is considered to have laid the foundation for the modern orchestra. Sometimes he placed as many as four (or more) groups of instruments and choirs, each complete in itself, in the galleries and balconies of St. Mark's Cathedral, resulting in colossal Baroque sound.

This great basilica with its Byzantine domes, its bronze horses, bright gold mosaics and immense interior bathed in greenish-golden light was the center of Venetian musical culture and its influence throughout Europe. The architectural concept of space-consciousness and echo effect is a key element in Baroque music, and it was developed at St. Mark's Cathedral. Gabrieli's "Sonata piano e forte" is the first score to indicate a change in volume dynamics.

It was traditional that European creative minds sought their final education in Italy. Robert Browning said that Italy was "his university," and it has been and is the university for many artistic people. Some of the students who stop at L'Abri Fellowship in Switzerland are coming from Florence or Venice or going there. In the same way that the great painter, Dürer, brought the Renaissance from Venice to Northern Europe, so did the music of Schütz show the mellowing influence of Italy.

Schütz studied in Italy for four years, and when Gabrieli died in 1612, Schütz returned to Germany. Gabrieli left his personal signet ring as a lasting token of friendship to his favorite pupil and Schütz passed on the great teaching he had received from Gabrieli to his many pupils. In a letter included in Moser's biography of Schütz, Schütz stresses the influence of his mentor: "Gabrieli—What a man he was . . . After I had been but a short time with my teacher, I found out how important and difficult was the study of composition . . . and I realized that I still had a poor foundation in it. From this time on I put away all my previous studies and devoted myself to the study of music alone. Upon the publication of my first humble work Giovanni Gabrieli urged me with great warmth to continue the study of music."

Schütz's studies with Gabrieli were important to the whole history of German music as Schütz was a major transmitter of the principals of the Venetian style to German composers.

Later Schütz made another trip to Venice to see Monteverdi who was the choirmaster of St. Mark's for 30 years and the most universal composer of the early Baroque. Dramatic conflict was the essence of Monteverdi's style. He used dissonance for dramatic expressiveness and believed that rhythm is bound up with emotion. He too had a strong influence on Schütz.

While Schütz was greatly influenced by his studies in Italy, his spiritual roots were in German soil. He was a devout Lutheran composer and is remembered not only for his universal culture and brilliant musical gift, but for his earnest biblical faith. Although he wrote the first German opera, *Dafne,* which is now lost, his enormous output is predominantly religiously inspired.

Schütz's first masterpiece in the "grand Italian manner" was his setting of *The Psalms of David* in 1619. He is often called the father of German music, and it is refreshing and enlightening to observe that he based his music almost exclusively on biblical texts. There is no "magic" in using Scripture, but when the words are believed by the artist there is bound to be a wholesome and healthy influence on those who listen to such music. Schütz had as his goal in composition to write the meaning of the words into the hearts of his hearers. Psalm 121 is an example of a superb union of words and music. It can well be said that Schütz unlocked the music hidden in the Psalms. He was the greatest composer of Psalm settings in the history of music. A special treasure is the Becker Psalter of 1628 including Schütz's plain four-part harmonic settings of the Psalms. The earnest simplicity which enhances religious music is felt in these settings.

The Magnificat was a favorite biblical passage of Schütz, and he composed several works to accompany it, including *The German Magnificat,* the last thing he wrote.

His most famous work of the oratorio type is *The Seven Last Words.* He was one of the earliest and among the greatest German composers of oratorio. An oratorio is distinguished from an opera by its sacred subject matter, and by the fact that oratorios were seldom, if ever, meant to be staged. The action is suggested or narrated, not presented. *The Seven Last Words* is a composite of all four Gospels. Schütz used the words of the Bible, and his oratorio presents the essence of Protestant thought. In describing pain he uses sharp dissonances. And again, because he wanted to convey the message, he is more interested in the clarity of the words than in counterpoint. He is a master of declamation. "Is there in the whole literature of music a more dramatic outcry than Schütz's treatment of the words 'My God, My God, Why hast Thou forsaken me?' " asks Moser. The quality of this fervent music sums up a quiet, yet deeply felt piety, a personal devotion before the Person of Christ. He used rests to focus the listeners' ears on certain passages. One critic called Heinrich Schütz the most spiritual musician the world has ever known. There is enduring vitality and biblical strength in his compositions.

Like Monteverdi, Haydn, and Verdi, Schütz wrote great music in his old age. He began to lose his hearing and sight, but in spite of these handicaps he created some of his finest music in this period. In 1664 he wrote the *Christmas Oratorio,* a brief biblical history, with Schütz's high-minded objective to intensify the effect of the Scriptures with music. He achieved his goal. All the words, which fit the music like a glove, are biblical except the beginning and the end. Schütz ends the oratorio this way:

"We give thanks to God, our Lord Christ, who by his birth hath enlightened us and by his blood hath redeemed us from the power of the devil. Let us all, with his angels, give praise to him with a loud voice, singing, Praise be to God in the highest."

Schütz wrote the greatest Passions of the 17th century. They are like the rest of his music, clean and pure, with a stress on content. These masterly works reveal Schütz as the greatest biblical composer of all time.

The influence of Schütz has been felt even into this century in the fine church music of the German composer, Hugo Distler. Every great artist is a part of his times, but because of the profound biblical content in his music, Schütz is for all time.

Schütz was the *Kapellmeister* (the Master of the Chapel) in Dresden from 1617 until the end of his life, except during some especially difficult years of the Thirty Years War when he was Court Conductor in Copenhagen.

When Schütz married in 1619 he combined invitations to his wedding with publication of his *Psalms of David.* The chapter of the Naumburg Cathedral on May 27 has in its minutes: "Heinrich Schütz, Electoral Saxon *Kapellmeister* in Dresden, sends the gentlemen a copy of his published *Psalms of David* and invites them to his wedding on June 1. The gentlemen vote that five Rhenish gold *guilden* be sent him as a honorarium, which they have taken from the large iron chest."

Schütz, with his gentle heart and spirit, was profoundly affected by the early death of his wife in 1625, and made a real decision before the Lord to spend the rest of his life in the composition of church music. He never remarried.

Schütz and the German people were deeply distressed by the long war, and in that tragic time found strength and comfort in Christian music. After the devastation of the war, Schütz helped with advice, money, and music to restore a number of musical establishments which had deteriorated.

Schütz died in 1672 and was buried in old Fraunkirche beside his wife. In the hall a brass tablet is inscribed, "The Christian Singer of Psalms—A joy for foreigners, for Germans a light."

Schütz is greatly loved, not only because of his music, but for his Christian way of life as well. Despite his many trials he never allowed his faith to waver. His great intelligence, personal integrity and staunch character earned him universal affection and esteem.

We learn from Schütz that choices are significant. He chose Christianity and dedicated his life to the praise of God, and his music did not suffer from the choice. God enhanced the talents of this gifted musician. Schütz also teaches us to learn from our "university" but to maintain a true biblical base for all learning; to turn to the Scriptures in hardships; and not to give up—even in old age.

Recommended Reading

Moser, Hans, *Heinrich Schütz: His Life and Work*. St. Louis: Concordia Publishing House, 1959.

Recommended Listening

Schütz: Christmas Oratorio
         Deutsches' Magnificat
         Psalms
         Seven Last Words from the Cross
Giovanni Gabrieli: Music for Organ and Bass
Monteverdi: Vespers

Chapter II
Antonio Vivaldi
(ca. 1678-1741)

"A merry heart doeth good like a medicine." Proverbs 17:22

The splendor and intensity of the musical life of Venice during the first part of the 18th century centered around Antonio Vivaldi. He has been described by Pincherle as "that whirlwind of music, perpetually pouring forth melodies, rhythms, harmonies, still as alive, for the most part, as on the day of their creation." Yet the music of this original composer, affectionately known as "Il Prete Rosso," because of his red hair and early training for the priesthood, was not heard for many years after his death in Vienna. He must have died poor and unknown as there is no trace of his grave. His music disappeared into obscurity, lying forgotten in public and private libraries. As Pincherle says, "Most forgotten composers deserve nothing better than to be forgotten . . . but now and then it happens that an obvious injustice is revealed."

A perusal of the latest *Schwann Catalog* proves that the

music of Vivaldi deserved to be resurrected. Currently there are over three pages devoted to Vivaldi recordings, with some concertos performed by 10 or 12 different artists. However, even the lively music of Vivaldi probably would have remained lost if Bach had not transcribed some of his works.

Bach was a victim of a fate similar to Vivaldi's. He too had slipped into oblivion. Then in 1829 the 20-year-old Mendelssohn introduced Bach's *Passion According to St. Matthew* to the music lovers of Berlin, and it met with tremendous success. The new admirers of Bach eagerly began to gather his scattered manuscripts. In the course of their research, someone came upon a score dating from 1739, entitled, "XII concerto [*sic*] di Vivaldi elaborati di J. S. Bach . . ." (Bach is known to have copied at least nine of Vivaldi's concertos.)

The natural question came to mind—Who was Vivaldi whom Bach had honored by transcribing his music? The "detectives" went to work, and finally a few original scores used by Bach were found in old engraved editions in an Amsterdam library. At first these originals were declared to be of slight value, but in the beginning of this century more enlightened scholars recognized Vivaldi as a powerful innovator, an inspired composer in his own right, and the actual creator of the solo concerto prefigured by Corelli and Torelli.

Antonio Vivaldi was born in Venice around 1678. He was the son of the leading violinist of St. Mark's Chapel. He was educated by his father and Legrenzi, who was the director of music at St. Mark's as well as a fine organist and composer. Vivaldi was trained for both music and the priesthood, and he became a priest in 1703. Because of ill health, he was excused from active service the following year, and afterwards devoted himself wholly to music.

Vivaldi became the head of the Conservatory of the Ospedale della Pietà which was a part of four institutions organized like convents and paid for by the state. They sometimes held as many as 6,000 orphan girls. Those admitted to the Pietà were generally illegitimate. Before the erection of these charitable institutions, Pincherle says "multitudes used to be found which had been thrown into the canals of the city." What was unusual about these semi-convents was that musical training formed an important part of the curriculum. In all music history there seems to be no parallel to the extent and quality of the music that rang through the corridors of the Ospedale della Pietà.

The girls were taught to sing, play the violin, the flute, the organ, the oboe, the cello, the bassoon. In short, there was no instrument, however unwieldly, that could frighten them. Music was the heart and soul of their lives. Every Sunday and on all holidays there were musical performances in the chapels by these young ladies, and about 40 of the best musicians would take part in each concert. All who wanted could attend the concerts, and they attracted large crowds. The people were allowed to stay as long as they remained in their seats. Applause was not permitted, and so instead there was coughing, loud nose-blowing, and much shuffling and stamping of feet. Many musicians, including Handel, commented on the excellence and liveliness of these performances. It was for these programs that Vivaldi wrote more than 400 concertos.

Wherever Vivaldi was there was abundant music making. In spite of his poor health, he was an incredible worker. Vivaldi was a progressive composer seething with ideas, and the Pietà was a wonderful environment to experiment with music. Vivaldi was a man of contrasts— quick to be irritated, quick to become calm. This characteristic is reflected in his music by dramatic contrasts of dynamics and harmony and varied rhythms, but the haste with which he composed was one of his weaknesses. There is much invention in Vivaldi's music and beautiful melodies, because he was always looking for new sounds. Vivaldi always had instruments and voices at hand to try out fresh ideas. ⌐

Venice in the 18th century was a life set to music like a perpetual opera. One is reminded of the wonderful contemporary paintings by Longhi with costumes and masks, all like a continual festival. In the daily life of Venice there was scarcely a time or place where the sound of music was not present. The Venetians had a mania for music which nearly consumed them.⌐

Vivaldi's career at the Pietà included teaching, composing, purchasing instruments, and conducting. Vivaldi, who was a violin virtuoso, was the soloist in the famous St. Mark's Cathedral. The Pietà where Vivaldi served nearly 40 years was located on the Riva degli Schiavoni a little before one reaches the Ponte del Sepolcro coming from St. Mark's. One of Canaletto's colorful paintings brings to mind what Vivaldi saw as he frequently walked from the Pietà along the Riva degli Schiavoni, past the Bridge of Sighs, turning at the Piazza (the center of Venice), looking at the magnificent Ducal Palace before entering St. Mark's Basilica to play his violin solo in the morning service. The Grand Canal with its myriad colors, the gondolas and gondoliers with their songs and the cheerful activity surely helped to fill Vivaldi's thoughts with bright sounds and melodies.

Canaletto (1697-1768), the first great chronicler of Venice, as a young apprentice assisted his father in painting theatrical scenes for several Vivaldi operas. Besides all his musical activity at the Pietà, Vivaldi wrote over 40 operas. Also he was allowed frequent leaves of absence to travel and conduct concerts elsewhere. Because of his poor health (it is thought that he suffered from asthma), he could never travel without a retinue of four or five people, which is a clue that he knew how to delegate some tasks into the hands of others; otherwise it is impossible to understand how he accomplished so much in the 63 or 64 years he was given in this life. Vivaldi's popularity today illustrates the truth that productivity is an integral part of greatness.

Vivaldi's European reputation was built on a set of 12 concerti grossi. A concerto grosso is a composition involving a few select soloists, usually three, and a full orchestra. A concerto involves one solo instrument and the orchestra. The Baroque idea of the instrumental sound of *solo-tutti* resulted in new sounds and contrasts. Vivaldi was the greatest Italian master of the concerto, and the influence of this original genius on future generations is incalculable. In the works of Vivaldi the concerto was definitely standardized as a cycle of three movements usually with a slow introduction. Vivaldi was the first to bring the pathos of Venetian opera arias into the slow movement of his concertos. He was also the first to give the slow movement the same importance as the fast movements. The performer was expected to add his own embellishments.

The two great Italian mediums were the voice and the violin. The violin comes closest to the sound of the singing voice and is capable of many possibilities. Every art depends on its means of expression, so it is no accident that the great Italian school of violin composition flourished at the time when Stradivari had found his own style of violin making. Antonio Stradivari (ca. 1644-1737) born in Cremona was the greatest of all violin makers. His violins are beautifully formed and perfect in every detail. This prodigious worker never repeated a design exactly, but always made some change seeking for perfection.

Another person important in relationship to the violin and the concerto grosso is Arcangelo Corelli (1653-1713). Born in Bologna, he spent his creative life in Rome and was one of the greatest of the early violinists. He is considered the founder of the modern method of violin playing and was also a noted teacher. He wrote no vocal music.

His interest was centered in string instruments. Corelli is considered the co-creator of the concerto grosso, and he had a strong influence on Vivaldi, Handel, and Bach. In fact, 18th century music was built on the foundation established by Corelli. His works were the fruit of slow and considered deliberation, and he had a noble concern for measure and balance. One of the great classicists, he and Vivaldi are incomparable masters of the string orchestra. Corelli lived simply and, like Handel, spent most of his money on paintings. He was calm, reflective, and cultured, contemplating his art with a religious respect. Music, painting, and friendship graced his life.

The Baroque period saw the development of the opera, the oratorio, the cantata, the creation of the solo sonata, the trio sonata, and the chamber duet. It instituted important forms of the concerto grosso and the solo concerto. The three central figures of the concerto are Corelli, Torelli, and Vivaldi. The Baroque composers wrote a great deal of music, because the public was ever clamoring for new works, so we can forgive these great composers if some of the vast output sounds stylized. Hardly any other age has been as prolific.

The Four Seasons is perhaps Vivaldi's most popular work. It is one of the masterpieces of descriptive music, and it left its mark on the musical life of Vivaldi's century. His style became the style of the moment. His bird sounds are as vivid as some of the wonderful bird mosaics in St. Mark's Cathedral. It is often performed today. Vivaldi, a poet full of lyrical power, wrote a sonnet for each of the seasons and the music to go with each season. *The Four Seasons* represents an important Baroque parallel to Haydn's oratorio, *The Seasons*. Later came Beethoven's *Pastoral Symphony*. Vivaldi is one of the towering figures in the transition from late Baroque to the early Classical style. Possibly the greatest paintings of the seasons are *Les Très Riches Heures* of the Duc de Berry.

Vivaldi, like his contemporaries, composed every work for a definite occasion—not simply "art for art's sake." He composed a great deal of music for plucked instruments, including the lute and guitar. His concertos for mandolin are delightful. We can always admire Vivaldi's seemingly inexhaustible creative power and vitality. His keen, often capricious, imagination finds external expression in the variety of instrumental combinations which reflect the Venetian fondness for coloristic effects. One can speak of Vivaldi's music as energetic, nimble, and full of life. Only a small part of his prolific production has been published.

His sacred works were written for the Pietà and hardly ever emerged from there. His splendid work, The Gloria in D, kindles a sense of rapture due to Vivaldi's own spiritual depth. Vivaldi often recited psalms and prayed out loud while walking in the corridors of the Pietà.

While listening to Vivaldi, do not forget that he was rediscovered after Bach's rediscovery. Vivaldi's music would have been lost to us if Bach had not learned by transcribing contemporary composers, especially the Italians. Today our problem is almost the opposite. We have too much available. One has a sense of bewilderment upon entering a music or book store or a library. How does one know what to listen to or to read? A good plan is to start with the best.

Vivaldi is among the best, but like all human beings he has his limitations too. After one listens to Vivaldi over a period of time one becomes aware of a sameness in the music. It does not have the depth and spiritual content of Bach; but it has life. It is never old music. When one turns to the radio and suddenly there is Vivaldi, his music brightens the room. When I open the shutters of Chalet Chesalet and see the sun rising above the Swiss Alps, listen to the singing of birds and the ringing of cow bells, I call it a "Vivaldi" day.

Recommended Reading

Pincherle, Marc. *Vivaldi: Genius of the Baroque.* New York: W. W. Norton, 1957.

Recommended Listening

Vivaldi: Concerto for Flute, Oboe and Bassoon
Concerto in C for Mandolin
Concerti for Recorder
Concerto for Two Trumpets
Concerti for Violin and Orchestra
The Four Seasons
Gloria in D
Pastor fido, Op. 13
Corelli: Concerto Grosso in G Minor
Op. 6, No. 8 *Christmas.*

Chapter III

Johann Sebastian Bach
(1685-1750)

"Praise Him with the sound of the trumpet: praise Him with the psaltery and harp. Praise Him with the timbrel and dance: praise Him with stringed instruments and organs." Psalm 150:3, 4

Johann Sebastian Bach, who may be described as a very determined person, was the outstanding member of the greatest musical family the world has ever known. The Thirty Years War was remembered by the Bach family because the Bach ancestors left Hungary rather than give up their biblical faith. The earliest musical Bach was a miller. When he went into the mill to grind his corn, regardless of the clatter of the mill-wheels, he would take along his zither and play it, foreshadowing the musical feelings of his descendants.

Bach and Handel were the culminating figures of the Baroque period (1600-1750) in music history. At this time Vivaldi was composing in Italy, Rameau was the court musician of Louis XIV in France, Handel was the central

41

figure in London, and Bach, known best as an organist in Germany, was creating a world of music. This period follows the Renaissance and Reformation, and the term "baroque" comes from the Portuguese word, *barroco,* meaning a pearl of irregular shape. The word baroque has long been used to denote the contemporary period of painting and architecture which includes the names of Rembrandt, Rubens, Velázquez, and Bernini.

It is valuable to examine the interrelationships of the creative activities of artists in the various areas, such as architecture, music, painting, poetry, and sculpture, as it helps us to understand and appreciate the other disciplines more deeply. As one takes time to study various artists which make up a period, one sees that the doors of the arts are constantly opening upon each other.

In the city of Eisenach, Germany, Johann Sebastian Bach was born on the first day of Spring, 1685. In the same city over 150 years earlier, Martin Luther had translated the Bible into German and also had written some of the hymns that were so essential in the music of Bach. Eisenach is also important to remember as the seat of the minnesingers, and where later Wagner used the Wartburg Castle for his opera, *Tannhäuser,* the very castle where Luther had translated the New Testament.

It can be said that if there had not been a Luther, there would not have been a Bach. The focus of Bach's spiritual life was in Christianity and in the service of religion through music. It is easy to pass over the statement I have just made and not realize the truth of the fact that Bach's Christian faith and his music are inseparably united. I have read countless contemporary books and various articles on Bach discussing the mystery of Bach's greatness, and the authors rarely mention his self-acknowledged indebtedness to his Lord and Savior. His belief in the reality of heaven caused his music to be timeless. As one critic said, "Without knowing it, he divided music history into two basic periods: pre-Bach and post-Bach. And in the post-Bach era he is a perpetual presence."

Bach spent his life in the musical service of God without being conscious of the extraordinary greatness of his work. In writing his music to the glory of God and doing his work as a conscientious craftsman who believes in doing a job well he undoubtedly would have been astonished to learn that over two hundred years after his death his compositions would be more often performed *and* studied, and his name more deeply respected by musicians than any other composer.

After the death of his parents, Bach at the age of ten went to live in Ohrduf with his elder brother who had been a student of Pachelbel. Johann Christoph was a good but stern teacher. He owned one volume of contemporary compositions that the young Bach was not allowed to use; and so over a period of six months, in the still of the night and by moonlight, he copied it all down. When the brother discovered it, he took away the manuscript, but Bach at this early age had begun a life-long habit of copying and learning from others. Unfortunately, however, this probably contributed to the eye strain which eventually led to his blindness.

After the death of his brother Bach was a boy soprano in Lüneberg for several years where he also went to school and came into contact with serious musical culture. There he distinguished himself as a violinist and viola player, and when he left Lüneberg, before he was 18-years-old, he also was recognized as a master clavichordist, organist, and a promising composer. He began his professional career playing violin and viola in the court orchestra at Weimar. He was not unhappy there, but the organ was his first love. Bach was next employed in Arnstadt where he wrote almost entirely organ music.

A major influence on Bach which helped to release his creative energies was his 200 mile walk in 1705 to hear the greatest organist of his generation, Dietrich Buxtehude. Buxtehude directed the *Abendmusiken* (evening musical devotions) in the cathedral of Lübeck. Much of Buxtehude's music was composed for these evening devotions which were held during the Advent season in Lübeck. Bach was almost fired because of his long absence, but his music was never the same afterwards. Buxtehude is in the unique position of being a link between the founder of Protestant Baroque music, Schütz, and its supreme master, Bach. All three of these great composers were Christians and knew and appreciated the Bible and its truthfulness.

Not only did Bach mature earliest in his organ compositions, but he was happiest at this noble instrument and remained absorbed in it throughout his career. During his lifetime he was known as a brilliant organist rather than as a composer, and his advice in organ building was sought all over Germany. In appraising an organ Bach always pulled out all the stops first to test the lungs of the instrument. Bach was praised for his performing ability, pedal technique, and art of registration. His habit of astonishing the congregation by trying unusual sounds on the organ stirred criticism, but it aided Bach's independent creative growth.

His next position was as organist in St. Blasius, Mülhausen, in 1707. There he married his cousin, Maria Barbara, who was also a musical Bach, and she bore him two of his famous musical sons, Wilhelm Friedemann and Carl Philipp Emanuel. Within less than a year he was back in Weimar as court organist to Duke Wilhelm Ernst. Here Bach reached his zenith as an organist.

The foundation of Bach's music was the German chorale. In Weimer he wrote some of his chorale preludes which are organ meditations on hymn tunes. Throughout Bach's life the Lutheran hymnbook was an unfailing stimulation for his genius. These great Reformation chorales were meant not to create a mood, but to convey a message. They were a confession of faith in the Scriptures, not simply personal feelings. Bach's first composition was a simple exercise on a hymn tune, and at the end of his life, he was still at work on a chorale, "Before Thy Throne I Now Appear."

The ideal of Bach was unity and diversity. His desire was to create unity yet with diversity in whatever he produced, and he found ways to tie together even the separate parts of a collection, most often by the use of familiar hymn tunes. His organ style was calculated to stimulate devotional feeling, and nowhere more so than in the *Orgelbüchlein*. In this wonderful "Little Book for the Organ," we feel the Dürer-like quality of his music. On the title page Bach wrote, "To the glory of God alone in the highest and to further the learning of everyone."

While in Weimar, Bach became interested in Italian music, especially that of Corelli and Vivaldi. His cousin, Walther, introduced him to the newest Italian music and he learned musical architecture from the Italians. The Bach style is really a fusion of Italian and German characteristics.

A man of strong opinions, Bach often had squabbles with those for whom he worked. Most often he was right. But the many struggles and hardships he had only drove him closer to his Lord. For example, when he was offered a better position in another city, the Prince in Weimar put Bach in prison for a month in order to keep him from leaving. Always an overcomer and an incredibly hard worker, Bach used this time to work on his *Orgelbüchlein*. Temperate, industrious, devout, Bach was a home lover and family man. He was genuine, hospitable, and jovial. Frugality and discipline ruled in the Bach home, but there was also unity, laughter, loyalty, and love. Bach was a very disciplined person who made the most of all the events—good and bad—in his life.

In 1717 Bach left Weimar and became the court conductor to the Prince of Cöthen. These years are known as the secular period of his life, because of the musicless atmosphere of the Calvinist Reformed church with which he was identified there. Like Rembrandt, Bach suffered under the control of the Calvinists, who believed that artistic music had no place in the church, and that it was not right for an artist to depict biblical scenes. But being in this position did not deter Bach who never shrank from the "impossible."

Even though we speak of this as his secular period, Bach did not shed his religion when he composed for secular purposes or for instruction. He did not write cheap or trivial works. He believed that the primary reason for music should be for the glory of God and the recreation of the mind. In Cöthen he wrote his central instrumental works including *The Well-tempered Clavier* (tempered means tuned) which revolutionized the tuning of instruments and is one of the most amazing works ever written. Along with Bach's other music it has had an enormous influence on such composers as Mozart, Beethoven, Mendelssohn, Chopin, Schumann, Brahms, and Hindemith. No composer has had an inventive faculty as profound and rich as Bach. He has been rightly spoken of as "a composer for all seasons."

In 1720 when Bach returned from a musical tour with the Prince, he was met at the door of his home with the shocking news that his wife was already dead and buried. His faith sustained him in this black hour. Later he married a soprano, Anna Magdelena, who was a superb helpmate to him, both in caring for the home and their children, and also musically. She helped to copy many of his manuscripts. For her beautiful soprano voice Bach wrote many of his most inspired arias. In all, Bach had 20 children, of whom 10 died in childhood. The youngest, Johann Christian, later became the famous "English" Bach composer.

From the music book Bach wrote for his wife, Anna Magdelena, he used a sarabande melody for his Goldberg

Variations. These were written for a wealthy man who suffered from insomnia. On the nights when he could not sleep, the gentleman would say to Bach's pupil, "Dear Goldberg, play me one of my variations." Everything Bach touched he improved. He did not invent anything, new, but it was the way he brought his many musical ideas together that made his music so rich. Many critics consider Bach the greatest of all composers. In him we have a supreme uniting of a person's faith and his talent. Cellist Pablo Casals who at 93 began his day by playing from *The Well-tempered Clavier* on the piano once said, "There is always something left to discover in it." Helmut Walcha, the blind German organist, added, "Ultimately Bach opens a vista to the universe. After experiencing him, people feel there is meaning to life after all."

The fusion of national styles in the unique Bach style is one of the most remarkable factors about his music. This merging of Italian, French, and German styles is most fully exemplified in his six *Brandenburg Concertos.* They continue the coloristic tradition of Venice and of Vivaldi's concertos. The wealth of counterpoint and variety of instrumental color make these concertos unique in this form. Bach loved the recorder and used it in the concertos. He felt its pure sound carried the soul's devotion to the throne of God. There is always a sense of direction in Bach's music. Even when it wanders, there is always a place of return and resolution.

After six years in Cöthen, Bach went to Leipzig in 1723. His crowning years of creativity were spent as cantor at the St. Thomas Church in Leipzig. It was here that he wrote a vast amount of vocal music, including the heart of his work, the cantatas. Of the nearly 300 cantatas that he composed, only about 200 survive today. Stravinsky once said that Bach's cantatas should be the heart of every musician's study. The cantatas join the Bible, music, and history into a unified whole. Rembrandt did the same in his etchings and paintings, expressing scriptural truth by means of great art.

Bach stressed the words and the message in his cantatas. One could do an entire study listening to passages which illustrate this. This same literalness can be observed in the 15 woodcuts of the Book of Revelation which are early masterpieces of the great Dürer. Bach, in a sense, placed himself "in the pulpit" to expound the Gospel, and his cantatas reflect the depth of Christianity. Bach wrote his music as an act of worship in the true mystical sense, and his faith and music are unified.

Along with the crystalline logic underlying all of Bach's works are the rhythms and controlled, but seeming spontaneous, harmonic modulations. One explanation as to why the music of Bach is popular today among young listeners is its living pulse. The pianist Glenn Gould has said, "There is a bridge between Bach's ideas of rhythm and those of the mid-20th century, and it has been created by popular music and jazz." That may or may not be true, but what eventually captivates the young listeners (according to a *Time* editorial) "is Bach's granite solidity that young people seem to respond to. It is as if he provided a firm ground-base for their improvisatory life-style." We can say as fellow believers with Bach that there is no "as if" about it. The firm base Johann Sebastian Bach has given to the world is Christianity.

Cantata No. 21, *I Was in Much Tribulation,* is in two sections. Part I depicts the sorrow and distress of the sinful soul, and Part II describes the spirit of rejoicing in the salvation brought by Jesus Christ. Bach also includes in this cantata one of his favorite hymns, "If Thou but Suffer God to Guide Thee." The final chorus of this cantata begins with a setting of the words, "Worthy Is the Lamb That Was Slain," which is strikingly similar to Handel's setting of the same text in his *Messiah.* Bach longed to know Handel whom he greatly admired, but they never met as

Bach traveled in a small radius within Germany, whereas Handel enjoyed cosmopolitan fame.

For years I have been giving Farel House lectures at L'Abri Fellowship. The first one I ever gave was on Bach cantatas. This was before the chapel when we had all meetings in the living room of Chalet les Mélèzes. After our neighbor and dear friend, Herr Lengacher, built our chapel, one of the first duets a friend and I performed was "Hasten to Jesus" from Cantata 78. As Tovey says, "Bach's Heaven always rests on a very solid foundation."* That foundation is Jesus Christ as truly God and truly man.

The culmination of Bach's work as a church musician were his *St. John* and *St. Matthew Passions.* Often he wrote on manuscripts, "With the help of Jesus," or "To God alone be the glory," acknowledging that his gift of music was from God. The *St. Matthew Passion* is considered one of the richest and noblest sacred works in existence. It is the creation of a mind intimately familiar and profoundly moved by the Gospel text. It is indeed one of civilization's incomparable masterpieces, and yet it was produced in the tense atmosphere of unfriendliness.

One critic said that Bach's move to Leipzig was a "monumental miscalculation." It is true that his salary and social status were lower than before, and also true that he entered into fresh difficulties with church officials and choir boys, but in God's overall plan for his life it was not a mistake. It is certain that Bach would not have written as much and as well and pioneered in almost every field of music if in these last years he had been famous and financially free to travel.

Bach in his old age did have one exciting triumph. He was invited to the court at Potsdam to play for King Frederick the Great of Prussia who was a gifted amateur musi-

*D. F. Tovey, *Essays in Musical Analysis* (London: Oxford University Press, 1946) p. 42

cian. Upon his arrival, the king dismissed everyone else, exclaiming, "Old Bach is here!" It was a memorable evening for the two of them with the musician delighting the king by improvising a fugue on one of Frederick's themes. Not too long after the court visit Bach's eyes began to fail, and after two operations which weakened him further, he died at 65, totally blind. While Bach lay upon his bed, shortly before his death, he dictated his last composition, the chorale, "Before Thy Throne I Now Appear."

Bach was mourned by many after his death, but only as a brilliant organist and teacher. Exactly 100 years after the first performance of the *St. Matthew Passion,* Mendelssohn, at the age of 20, resurrected it. The 1829 performance was received with enthusiasm and awe. Mendelssohn helped to establish Bach's place in the musical world, but in all likelihood, no other age than our own has better appreciated the true nature of Bach's wide-ranging giftedness. We have benefitted today from the research done by eminent musicologists who have brought the works of Bach into clearer focus, and the advent of records has created a vast new audience for Bach by making available countless Bach albums. According to the *Bach-Werke-Verzeichnis (BWV),* Bach wrote more than 1,000 works of which nearly three-quarters were intended to be performed at Christian worship services.

Bach's influence in music history has been one of health and strength. He is difficult to perform, but he never wrote empty virtuosity. His music has content. Another of his sublime works, the B Minor Mass, with its monumental choruses, was written for the church universal with a thoroughly Protestant spirit. Bach considered the German mass as arranged by Luther as a memorial and not a sacrifice. The B Minor Mass has only one companion, and that is Handel's *Messiah.* The aim of both creations is the artistic presentation of the essence of Christianity, Handel writing from the historical viewpoint and Bach from the doctrinal.

Bach, a true mystic in the proper biblical sense, lived life to the fullest. Yet he understood that our days upon this earth are numbered. In "Come Sweet Death" Bach expresses the height and depth of his faith. Einstein says, "It can fairly be said that no composer thought more about death or stood in greater awe of it than Bach. Bach welcomed death, although he feared it; and between his fear and his longing stood only an indomitable and rock-like faith." Johann Sebastian Bach was one of the spiritually wisest musicians the world has known.

From Martin Luther's choice to stand for the truth of Scripture and by surrounding himself with artists, poets, musicians, philosophers, and theologians, the Reformation reached into every realm of culture. Few in our age have even dreamed of, let alone put into practice, such possibilities—based on a clear understanding of Christianity—the way Bach, Schütz, Handel, Dürer, Rembrandt, and Milton did. As Machen said, "The vast majority of those who reject the gospel do so simply because they know nothing about it. But whence comes this indifference? It is due to the intellectual atmosphere in which men are living. The modern world is dominated by ideas which ignore the gospel. Modern culture is not altogether opposed to the gospel. But it is out of all connection with it. It not only prevents the acceptance of Christianity. It prevents Christianity from getting a hearing."*

As it will often be expressed in these pages: "We need to go back in order to go forward." Listen to Bach, appreciate the richness and diversity of his music, but hear his message too.

---

*J. G. Machen, *Christianity and Culture* (Huémoz, Switzerland, L'Abri Fellowship, 1969) p. 8

Recommended Reading

David, Hans T. and Mendel, Arthur (eds.). *The Bach Reader: A Life of Bach in letters and documents.* New York: Norton, 1945.

Field, Laurence N. *Johann Sebastian Bach.* Minneapolis: Augsburg Publishing House, 1943.

Geiringer, Karl. *Johann Sebastian Bach: The Culmination of an Era.* London: Allen and Unwin, 1967.

Newman, Werner. *Bach, A Pictorial Biography.* London: Thames and Hudson, 1961.

Recommended Listening

6 Brandenburg Concertos
Cantatas: No. 4 *Christ Lay in the Bonds of Death*
          No. 21 *I was in Much Tribulation*
          No. 80 *A Mighty Fortress is Our God*
          No. 106 *God's Time is the Best Time*
          No. 140 *Wake! Awake!*
          No. 211 *Coffee Cantata*
Chorale Preludes: Orgelbüchlein
                 Christmas Oratorio
                 Goldberg Variations for Harpsichord
                 Magnificat in D
                 Mass in B Minor
                 St. John Passion
                 St. Matthew Passion
                 Toccata and Fugue in D Minor
                 Well-tempered Clavier
                 Jesu Meine Freude (Motet)
                 Four Orchestral Suites

Chapter IV
George Frideric Handel
(1685—1759)

"This noble prince of music."—Lang

"If an artist could live to read his biography," says Lang, "he would recognize not so much himself as the mask that covered his face." But I do not believe Handel would mind too much what we say about him, as long as we listen to his music. He said very little about himself in his lifetime. The central fact of his life was his music. He would be happy to know what joy and pleasure his music, particularly *Messiah,* gives to so many people, but would probably be surprised at how little of his music is known today. Handel had an immense genius. The magnitude of his gift from God, and the avalanche of great music he wrote, is scarcely suspected in this generation except by musical experts.

George Frideric Handel was born in Halle, Germany, within a month of Bach. His father, a barber-surgeon, was a strong individual with an acute business sense and a desire for his son to be a lawyer. His mother, the daughter of a Lutheran pastor, was a good and pious lady and Handel had deep respect and affection for her all his life.

The musical gifts of Handel must have been noticed early, but his father paid no attention to such "frivolities" as music. When George Frideric was eight or nine, the Duke of Weissenfels heard him play the postlude to a church service and he summoned the boy's father and told him he ought to encourage such talent. As Handel's father was the surgeon of the court, there was nothing to do but give in, and Handel began studying music instead of law.

His only teacher was Friedrich Wilhelm Zachow, a most learned and imaginative musician and teacher, who instilled in his young pupil a lifelong intellectual curiosity. Zachow gave Handel instruction in organ, harpsichord, violin, and oboe (Handel learned to love the oboe, and years later in his famous *Fireworks Music* used 24 oboes!). Handel also received from Zachow a solid grounding in harmony, counterpoint, choral writing, and imaginative orchestration. When he was 11, he wrote his first composition, and he played the organ well enough to substitute for his teacher when needed. Handel's appreciation for his instructor knew no end, and after Zachow died in 1712, Handel sent frequent gifts to his widow. Remembering widows and orphans was characteristic of Handel throughout his life. He was a charitable man and very fond of children.

When Handel was 17 or 18, he went to Hamburg. Newman Flower says that the musician left Halle aimlessly to find fortune. Not so. I agree with Lang who declared that George Frideric Handel never crossed a street aimlessly. As we have seen many talented people come to L'Abri Fellowship over the years for direction in their lives, having criss-crossed Europe and the Middle East after graduating from college, so did Handel go to Hamburg in 1703 to begin his "great search" how to work out the ideas flooding his mind. And there in Hamburg he discovered opera with its amalgamation of French, German, and Italian styles. In two years he produced his first opera, *Almira,* and now having somewhat of a reputation, he went to Italy, "the promised land of musicians."

There are pages we could write about the fertile Italian period, 1706 to 1710, but this at least must be said. While in Rome in 1708 Handel wrote the oratorio, *The Resurrection.* It was his first notable religious effort, and he composed it in a month. It was performed under the direction of Corelli. Corelli, who was highly respected in Western Europe, was the great conservative musician of Italy, and he had a profound influence on Handel. Corelli was a meticulous, critical, and gifted musician, and through his diligence he summed up everything that a century of instrumental music had produced. None of it was lost on Handel. The second opera Handel wrote in Italy, *Agrippina,* was performed in Venice in 1709, and it achieved such a sensational success that Handel, the Saxon Lutheran, became one of the most noted composers in Italy. The Venetians loved him, and spoke of him as "il caro Sassone" (the dear Saxon), and his triumph in Venice brought him world fame, as any successful Venetian production immediately made the rounds of the Italian operatic dependences abroad. In his stay in Venice, Handel and Domenico Scarlatti, one of Italy's most important harpsichord composers, became close friends.

Handel wrote little in Venice, but favors were heaped upon him, and here the deciding factor in his life was his meeting the brother of the future King George I of England. The younger brother invited Handel to come to Hanover where he obtained the post of musical director, but it was only an episode, because almost immediately he was off on a long leave of absence to London, where his sparkling opera *Rinaldo* made a success. Back to Hanover he went, and finally in 1712 he moved to England and remained there the rest of his life.

Two factors caused Handel's creativity to soar in Eng-

land. The country was a beehive of musical activity with
Italian opera ruling the day, and within the next 30-year
period, Handel wrote about 40 operas. He understood
the voice wonderfully as a result of his years in Italy. The
second reason was that the Elector of Hanover became
King George I of England in 1714, and the German-born
Handel, after the new King forgave him for leaving his
post in Hanover, won favor at court. Handel wrote his
Water Music Suite hoping for the King's pardon, and with
such glorious music he quickly received it.

Handel's years in Italy were very important to him.
Handel was always interested in melody and beautiful
sound (euphony)—the supreme Latin ideal. He retained
this all his life. No German surpassed him in writing beautiful melodies. But we must hold in balance the truth that
the Baroque was the great period of Protestant music, and
of course, we know that the Protestant culture was rooted
in the Bible.

Both Bach and Handel learned, borrowed, and copied
from great men like Corelli and Vivaldi and others, but
they were constantly experimenting, inventing, and always
giving their music their singularly sure touch. As Grout
explains for the benefit of those who belittle Handel for
his eclecticism: "Most of his borrowings were from his own
earlier works, but a considerable number were from other
composers . . . If he borrowed, he more often than not
repaid with interest, clothing the borrowed material with
new beauty and preserving it for generations that otherwise would scarcely have known of its existence."

Handel is really the inventor of the organ concerto with
orchestral accompaniment. These original concertos with
their warm, expressive melodies are uncomplicated, popular concert music in the best sense of the word. Handel
found his way to the heart of the world by the understanding of simple things. In his oratorios, there are simple
things, as well as sumptuous Venetian double choruses. A

secret of great art is to have contrast. A good illustration is Handel's *Messiah* with its majestic choruses and sudden dramatic silences.

Handel's music is as much Italian as it is German. In fact, Handel is the international composer. There is also a sense of French "grandeur" in his music, and England provided him with the choral tradition. Handel, indeed, may be spoken of as a citizen of the world, whereas Bach remained in Germany all his life. Yet under the hand of God, both men are great composers. It should be an encouragement to all of us to be creative with what we have where we are.

Handel was the man of action, the extrovert, the improviser. While he was still in Italy, he was looking ahead and obtained most of his best singers for his operas written and performed in England. Bach was also a skillful improviser, but he wished to bring each detail to perfection, whereas Handel desired to make an overall big effect on his listeners. Handel matured earlier than Bach, and both composers, as we said, appropriated the best from other artists and made the music even better.

Something must be said about Handel the man and why he was an inviting target for critics and for satire. He was a foreigner, and an individual *no one* could help noticing. He had large hands, large feet, a large appetite, and he wore a huge white wig with curls rippling over his shoulders. He spoke English rather loudly in a colorful blending of Italian, German, and French.

He was tempermental, he loved freedom, and he hated restrictions which placed limits on his art. Like Bach, he was often at variance with others. But in his most dramatic fits of agitation there was no real malice, and these scenes frequently were extremely comical. Handel had the gift of command, and even in violent situations (and unless you have been in the theater you do not know how violent it can be at rehearsals and backstage!), through wisdom and his sense of humor, he had the power of healing wounds.

One evening in an opera performance being played before the Princess of Wales and other noble persons, two prima donnas, in a moment of jealousy, seized one another by the hair. This extra "act" brought forth roars of laughter. Later a farce was written which dramatized this historic "battle of temperament" and the author gave the victory to Handel who walked over to the percussion section of the orchestra and with several blows on the kettledrum brought the struggle to an end.

Between 1718 and 1720, Handel lived on the estate of the Duke of Chandos where he was master of the duke's chapel. Here he composed the Chandos Anthems which are Psalm settings. They laid the cornerstone for his future choral compositions. These were the most carefree years of Handel's life. After this interval in the country he moved back to London, and for the next 17 years he helped to manage the Royal Academy of Music, as well as compose and produce operas.

When Handel first arrived in England, the use of English librettos in the operas had been already abandoned without a murmur; but finally the English people wearied of Italian operas, and Handel gradually began to compose oratorios in English. His first success was *Esther*.

When one speaks about famous people and their successful lives often the detail of their suffering, anguish, and day-by-day struggles is passed over lightly. It is not fair to do this to anyone, and in particular to Handel. His London years were up and down, and unbelievably down at times. As Romain Rolland has tried to explain it: "He was surrounded by a crowd of bulldogs with terrible fangs, by unmusical men of letters who were likewise able to bite, by jealous colleagues, arrogant virtuosos, cannibalistic theatrical companies, fashionable cliques, feminine plots, and nationalistic leagues. . . . Twice he was bankrupt, and once he was stricken by apoplexy amid the ruins of his company. But he always found his feet again; he never gave in."* Handel, the sanest of geniuses was a hand-breadth from insanity. More than once even his friends thought that he had lost his reason; but no matter how difficult his life really was, Handel, the musician, escaped from his trials into the serenity of his art. In this realm he had supreme self-control.

Few suspected his nervous tension and the depth of his emotion when he was exalted by transports of joy, fury, enthusiasm, or overwhelming sadness. When Handel was writing *Messiah,* which he put down on paper in 24 days without once leaving his house, his servant brought him food, and when he returned, the food was often un-touched. While working on the "Hallelujah Chorus," his servant found him with tears in his eyes. He exclaimed, "I did think I did see all Heaven before me, and the great God Himself!"

Because Handel lived fully with his heart, his suffering was deep, but out of it came his great music. His power to create a mood with overwhelming poetic depth and suggestiveness is unrivaled. Lesser men who did not un-derstand his genius enjoyed satirizing him as a glutton and a tyrant, but the truth is his strong personality (with its rougher aspects) was balanced by a sense of humor, his generosity and honesty, his sincere piety, and his super-human determination.

The music of Handel is lively, because he was full of life, and it is intimate, yet universal. Always he wrote for his immediate audience, but because there is a timelessness about his music, we are able to appreciate him today.

He drew his music from everywhere. He once told a friend that he got inspiration for some of his airs from the street cries of London. It reminds one of Charles Dickens who received an important part of his education while

*R. Rolland, *Essays on Music,* edited by D. Ewen (New York: Dover Publications, Inc., 1959) p. 218

walking the streets in London. Into the atmosphere of a big, noisy city, Handel brought the beauty of the country. One of his masterpieces "L'Allegro ed il Penseroso" with words by John Milton is filled with imaginative musical nature painting. His music is healthy and communicative. One feels his optimism in his great choruses. His music is among the most noble ever written, and yet it was misunderstood by church people at first, because his biblical oratorios were performed in theaters.

The use of biblical words in a theater was revolutionary, and those who opposed Handel went to great extremes to keep his oratorios from being successful. For example, certain self-righteous women gave large teas or sponsored other theatrical performances on the days when Handel's concerts were to take place in order to rob him of his audience, or his enemies hired boys to tear down the advertisements of his concerts.

It is true that Handel hated restrictions and avoided as many official appointments as he could. He took no pains to humor socially minded people, and he had no respect for his unmerciful critics. He was an artist, and he did not alter his God-given ideas to please others. Such a man as George Frideric Handel was not likely to please women, and he troubled his mind very little about them. But I must say quickly that Handel was not unsociable or irresponsible. He simply knew what had to come first. Though he never married, he was not without devoted friends and companionship. Some of his friends were among the noblest intellects of the age.

Two of Handel's greatest oratorios, *Saul* and *Israel in Egypt,* were written in four months, the autumn of 1738, when he was 53 years old. He leased a theater to perform these oratorios during Lent, and as an added attraction, he improvised at the organ during the intermission. To appreciate the greatness of Handel and his ability to overcome, keep in mind the fact that one year before he wrote

Saul and *Israel in Egypt,* he had suffered a paralytic stroke and a nervous collapse. And then when you listen to *Israel in Egypt,* also remember that its first performance was an outright failure, and it was not performed again for 17 years; in fact, it never was a success in Handel's lifetime.

Israel in Egypt contains some of his most sublime inspiration. He is at his finest in the choruses. Handel was the master of the basic Baroque principle of contrast which makes his music so lively and interesting. Much 20th-century music is extremely dull because of the lack of variety.

To better appreciate the music of Handel one must understand that he was an art collector. He owned some paintings by Rembrandt, and he delighted in wandering through art museums. One can see the large man with his enormous hands and feet studying a painting with intensity, undoubtedly talking out loud to himself, with more people looking at him than at the paintings on the wall. Because of his interest in art, his music is intensely visual. Handel was like a painter who was at his best in gigantic mural frescos.

In *Israel in Egypt,* there is a description in music of the plagues sent by God upon the Egyptians. One hears (and practically sees) the hopping of frogs, the arrival of all manner of flies and lice, and the locusts without number which devoured the fruits of the ground. The beginning of the hail storm is unforgettable, and the quietness when the chorus sings, "He sent a thick darkness over the land, even darkness which might be felt." It is musical tone painting at its greatest.

Good poetry, and particularly the words of Scripture, always attracted the composer. He was thoroughly familiar with his Bible, and he probably selected the words for *Israel in Egypt.* The words come mainly from Exodus and the historical psalms. In the chorus, "But as for His People," Handel gives other Christians the courage to believe in the power of God to do what He says He will do for His people.

Probably the Wesley brothers knew Handel. In the hymnal *Christian Praise,* there is one superb hymn, "Rejoice, the Lord is King," with words by Charles Wesley and music by George Frideric Handel.

Handel composed the *Messiah* in 1741 at the age of 56, and as Newman Flower observes, "Considering the immensity of the work, and the short time involved in putting it to paper, it will remain, perhaps forever, the greatest feat in the whole history of musical composition." As we marvel at it, let us not forget to listen to the message. When Handel finished his masterpiece, he put it in a drawer. He did not intend to produce it in London, having been through such turmoils over his other oratorios. But then came an invitation from Dublin, and in the society of cheerful Irishmen, Handel began to recover his good spirits.

The *Messiah* was first performed in Dublin in 1742, and immediately won huge popular success. When a nobleman complimented Handel on the great entertainment of the *Messiah* Handel replied, "My Lord, I should be sorry if I only entertained them; I wished to make them better." And better we are because of Handel's *Messiah,* particularly if we too believe the message.

The proceeds went to three charitable undertakings. This was nothing new with Handel. He was always generous. He had his faults, but there was nothing mean nor small in him. When he was poor, he was liberal, and when he became rich, he remembered his friends and those in need. He had a particular interest in the Society of Musicians (like Verdi's "Casa Verdi") and the Foundling Hospital. Whenever the *Messiah* was performed afterwards, it was almost entirely reserved for the benefit of charity.

In 1751 when Handel began to write the chorus that ends the second act of *Jephtha,* he noted at the bottom of the page that he was prevented from continuing the work because of "the relaxation of the sight in my left eye." Later when he learned he was really going blind, it was the lowest moment in his life. He had no fear of the coming darkness, but he dreaded the termination of his work. It nearly crushed him, but after awhile he struggled through to the end of *Jephtha.*

When he no longer could see to compose, he returned to playing. He practiced the harpsichord for hours each day, and having a dread of idleness, he began to organize performances. Also he still appeared on Sundays as a regular worshiper at St. George's in Hanover Square.

In 1759 when the oratorio season opened in March, Handel announced a series of 10 concerts. The almost blind composer conducted all of them, and on the 6th of April, shortly before Easter, was the performance of his *Messiah.* He carried it through to the end without seeming fatigue, but he knew his time to leave this world was soon to come. He told some friends that he had one desire—to die on Good Friday. "I want to die on Good Friday," he said, "in the hope of rejoining the good God, my sweet Lord and Saviour, on the day of His resurrection." Shortly before his death a very special person, Selina Hastings, Countess of Huntingdon, visited him at his request. Lady Huntingdon was a true Christian, a remarkable individual, and a generous supporter of Wesley and Whitefield.

When the morning of Good Friday arrived, Handel bade farewell to his friends, and then told his servant not to admit anyone else, because as he said, "I have now done with the world." He died on April 14, 1759, and was buried in Poets' Corner in Westminster Abbey. There are two verses in Scripture that come to my mind when I think of George Frideric Handel: "A just man falleth seven times and riseth up again" (Proverbs 24:16), and "When I sit in darkness, the Lord shall be a light unto me" (Micah 7:8).

Handel did not like to traffic in miniatures. Everything was big with him, including his heart. In all his nobility, he could not do things in small, timid ways. His life was rich in melody, and he poured it out generously. Most 20th-century composers have lost the sense of beauty. One hears few pleasant sounds today. That is why many sensitive, artistic people have turned back and listen to Baroque music; it is beautiful, and we have a need for beauty in our lives. Handel has spaciousness in his music, a marvelous sense of timing. His dramatic silences are full of awe. Much modern music batters the listener and adds to the noise and confusion in our already noisy and confusing lives. The music of Handel helps to bring order and joy into living.

In our enthusiasm for *Messiah* we should not neglect some of the other great oratorios. He wrote 26. But let us never cease to marvel at the mighty Handelian hammer strokes on the words, "Wonderful, Counsellor, the Mighty God," and the contrast and truth of the words, "He was despised." Also his organ music is marvelous. May this chapter serve as a brief introduction to my favorite composer.

Recommended Reading

Lang, Paul Henry. *George Frideric Handel.* New York: W. W. Norton, 1966.

Flower, Newman. *George Frideric Handel: His Personality and His Times.* New York: Charles Scribner's Sons, 1948.

Recommended Listening

L'Allegro ed il Penseroso
Chandos Anthems
Concerti Grossi (op. 3 and 6)
Concerto in B Flat for Harp and Orchestra
Concerti for Organ

Dettingen Te Deum
Israel in Egypt
Judas Maccabaeus
Messiah
Royal Fireworks Music
Saul
Solomon
Water Music

Chapter V
Franz Joseph Haydn
(1732—1809)

"God gave me a cheerful heart, so He will surely forgive me if I serve Him cheerfully."—Haydn

Franz Joseph Haydn was one of the sanest, most productive composers in history. His music is played nearly every day over the Swiss FM radio, and I believe there are specific reasons why he still is popular. The music of Haydn has cheer, beauty, logic, order, nobility, freshness of imagination, and humor. These are foreign words to our whole modern climate.

Haydn was in his twenties when Jean Jacques Rousseau was recklessly urging people to throw over ancient habits and laws, and demanding absolute freedom for the individual. Rousseau's *Discourse on the Origin of Inequality* excited many intellectuals, students, and artists of the 18th century and was enthusiastically accepted by many of them, but not by Franz Joseph Haydn. He was a man who respected God and the order in His creation, and he saw beyond the momentary "excitement" of violently changing

67

the present political, religious, and educational system without putting into the void a real base which is found only in true Christianity. Those who deny the truth of Scripture never find freedom.

Haydn accepted his life, hard as it was at times, and found it good. He recognized that there are fresh possibilities ahead for those willing to be builders in life rather than destroyers. Haydn wrote some of his richest and happiest music toward the end of his life. He said on one occasion, "God gave me a cheerful heart, so He will surely forgive me if I serve Him cheerfully." He said that often when obstacles came into his life and he found it hard to persevere, something within him whispered, "There are but few contented and happy individuals here below; everywhere grief and care prevail; perhaps your labor may one day be the source from which the weary and worn, or the person burdened with affairs, may derive a few moments of rest and refreshment." He wrote that in a letter to a group of enthusiastic music lovers who got together in the small German town of Bergen and performed his *Creation,* and had written to tell him how delighted and thankful they were for his music. And some 200 years later many of us also are glad Haydn persevered and left to us, as a legacy, his cheerful music. We delight in the truthfulness of his merry and unequivocal temperament.

Haydn was born in 1732 and raised in a humble but music-loving family in the village, Rohrau, in Lower Austria. The parents instilled their children with a love of work, method, and cleanliness, and above all, a respect for religion. As a boy Haydn spent nearly all his time in church and school.

He left home at the age of six for musical training, and when he was eight years old he became a choir boy in Vienna. He stayed at the school for nine years, acquiring enormous practical knowledge of music by constant performances, but to his disappointment, he received too little instruction in music theory. Always full of humor and pranks, Haydn could not resist cutting off the pigtail of a fellow singer. He was put out of the choir because of this incident, but more likely the real reason was that his voice had changed.

For a period of time the 17-year-old Haydn had a meager existence giving lessons and playing night serenades in the streets of Vienna. But he had already set his heart and mind on a life of music regardless of difficulties, and with unusual calmness in an artistic temperament, he persevered through several years of poverty. Thanks to tremendous persistence Haydn mastered counterpoint and gradually made himself known to certain influential persons in Vienna. Nicola Porpora, the famous Italian composer and singing teacher, gave him a few lessons in composition. At one time Haydn accompanied the pupils of Porpora and lived in the Michaelerhaus in Vienna. As an opera singer I studied in this same building some 200 years later to prepare to sing Brünnhilde in Wagner's *Die Walküre.*

Because Haydn did prevail over his hardships with stubborn tenacity and resourcefulness he became one of the most independent spirits in musical history, and one of the most deliberate and disciplined. He always found composition a labor, and so he set for himself regular hours to compose. When ideas did not come, he prayed for them. When they came, he worked with unremitting industry.

His 40-year childless marriage was no joy to either partner. Haydn's wife did not understand music and showed no interest in her husband's work. It was reported that she used his manuscripts for pastry linings or curl paper. In 1761 Haydn was appointed the musical director in the country home of Prince Paul Esterhazy, which involved a multitude of activities. Haydn carried out these duties extremely well. His service as chief of personnel revealed tact, good nature, and skill in dealing with people. Living in the country was no hardship for his contented disposition. He loved hunting, fishing, and other outdoor activities. Here he served nearly 30 years under circumstances which were ideal for his development as a composer. There was always something musical going on at the Esterhazy estate. The Hungarian Prince loved music and was a bountiful patron. As Haydn once explained, "I was cut off from the world; there was no one to confuse or torment me, and I was forced to become original."

We have somewhat the same environment at L'Abri. It is true that we are here to be a shelter to other people, but it has turned out that living in a small, mountain village has been a shelter and a stimulus for some of us interested in the arts. We too have been forced to be creative under the leadership of God.

Besides his many operas, Haydn wrote for all kinds of instruments. Our Christmas record has Haydn's charming flute-clock pieces played on the Flentrop organ. Haydn is often referred to as the Father of the symphony and the string quartet as we know them today. The quartet was his natural way of expression—organized simplicity. His quartets are clear, logical, and cheerful compositions.

One writer declared that after listening to Haydn, he always felt impelled to do some good work. This observation could not be made about many 20th-century composers. They more often irritate the listener, occasionally enrage him. But I find that after the first shock of hearing Berio, Stockhausen, or Boulez, I become quickly bored, and *never* have I felt like doing a good work after listening to John Cage.

In talking about Haydn it is impossible to leave out Mozart who was 24 years younger than Haydn. It was he who gave him the nickname, "Papa Haydn." They first met in 1781, and a deep friendship followed with both composers learning from one another. Haydn's best symphonies were written after he met Mozart. Their friendship was one of the rare instances of complete and mutual understanding between two musicians, entirely free from jealousy, each one appreciating the abilities of the other.

About 10 years later, when Haydn was invited to go to London, Mozart wrote to him, "Dear Papa, You were never meant for running around the world, and you speak too few languages." Haydn replied, "The language I speak is understood by the whole world." And off to London he went. It did prove to be a fruitful time, and he was right. The language he "spoke" is understood by the whole world. It was a good moment in Haydn's life, but also a sad time as he never saw his younger friend again. Mozart died at the age of 35 in 1791.

Haydn's success in England was immediate and emphatic. He left London, happy, prosperous, and internationally famous. Indeed, he became the most beloved composer of his time. His truly remarkable fund of musical ideas, his wealth of invention and the amazing clarity of his works are as fresh today as when he wrote them.

Haydn's 12 London symphonies are the crown of his achievement and the works of a consummate master. All that he had learned in 40 years of composing went into them, but even so, he remained an entertainer. He was not so concerned with making the world better but happier. His best known work in this group is the *Surprise* Symphony. The title comes from the andante movement where there is a surprise chord to wake up the audience. Haydn said that it would make all the women scream. Jokes came naturally to Haydn because of his inherent good nature.

The *Clock* Symphony with its iron logic and coherence is unsurpassed, and *La Poule* (the Chicken Symphony)is charming, amusing music. It received its name from a peculiar cluck in the second theme. The first theme sounds like a rooster chasing a hen, and in the last fugal movement, there is the laying of a prize egg. Cheerful and childlike, Haydn wanted to make people smile, not to add to their hardships and agonies.

The Creation is an oratorio which was inspired as a result of Haydn hearing a mighty performance of Handel's *Messiah*. He was stunned and thrilled with the music and the words and awed at the way it was received by the audience with absolute storms of applause. While composing *The Creation* Haydn told his biographer, "Daily I fell on my knees and asked God for strength." The words are taken from John Milton's writings and from the Bible. One of the sublime moments is the climax of the chorus, "And There Was Light." It is an unforgettable, overwhelming fortissimo.

Also in his last years Haydn wrote the oratorio, *The Seasons*. It is delightful, pleasing music with charming descriptions of nature, expressing man's innocent joy in the simple natural life. Certainly Bach and Handel had a clearer Christian witness than Haydn, but one senses the Christian base behind his works. When the Emperor asked Haydn which oratorio he preferred, Haydn said, *"The Creation.* Because in *The Creation* angels speak, and their talk is of God. In *The Seasons* no one higher than Farmer Simon speaks."

In 1808 Haydn was brought on a stretcher to hear a performance of *The Creation* in Vienna where he spent his last years. At the glorious moment when the chorus sings "And There Was Light," the audience burst into applause. Haydn was heard to say with trembling hands uplifted, "Not from me. It all comes from Above."

The Austrian national hymn, "Glorious Things of Thee Are Spoken," was written by Haydn, and the words are by John Newton. The tune is to be found in the second movement of his *Emperor* Quartet. Haydn played it often, and it was the last thing he heard before his death. Again and again in his last days he expressed the hope, "not wholly to die; but to live on in my music." God has surely answered his prayers.

An entertaining as well as instructive game to play is to turn on the FM radio and attempt to identify the piece of classical music being played. So that you will become a skillful listener, here are some suggestions to help you:

1. First try to distinguish the period (Is it Baroque, Classic, Romantic, Impressionist, Modern?)

2. Next, What instruments are used? (Decide whether it is a symphony, a song, opera, piano concerto, quartet, or otherwise.)

3. If still bewildered, try to identify what nationality is being expressed in the music.

4. Is the composition written by a major composer? Remember that the great composers have a style of their own.

a) Try to name the composer, narrowing it down perhaps to Haydn, Mozart, or Beethoven.

b) If there is a soft, singing passage followed by a very loud chord, it is probably Beethoven. (Remember what Renoir said, ". . . he doesn't spare us either the pain in his heart or the pain in his stomach.")

5. After careful listening, attempt to name the specific piece.

Obviously this game may be played in your home or in a classroom by having one person select records and having the listeners guess what is being played.

Recommended Reading

Geiringer, Karl. *Haydn, A Creative Life in Music.* Berkeley: University of California Press, 1968.

Hughes, Rosemary. *Haydn.* New York: Collier Books, 1963.

Recommended Listening

Concerti for Organ
Serenade Quartet Op. 3, No. 5
Emperor Quartet Op. 76, No. 3
The Creation

The Seasons
Farewell Symphony No. 45
Hunt Symphony No. 73
La Poule Symphony No. 83
Surprise Symphony No. 94
Military Symphony No. 100
Clock Symphony No. 101
Mass No. 9 in D Minor—*Nelson Mass*

Chapter VI
Wolfgang Amadeus Mozart
(1756—1791)

"His music seemed to come out of an ideal realm undisturbed by the troubles of life."—Grout

Wolfgang Amadeus Mozart, born in Salzburg, was probably the most sheerly musical composer who ever lived. Whenever Goethe spoke of the nature of genius, he would speak about Mozart who appeared to him as "the human incarnation of a divine force of creation." Mozart had the single-mindedness of genius. He seemed born to create music. Indeed, his gift of writing music was like a cosmic phenomenon. At times he appeared to be like a human computer. From the age of four until he died at the age of 35, he scarcely had a day's rest. Mozart wrote so much music that one can hardly hope to hear more than half of it in a lifetime of listening.

His thoughts were always occupied with music, and with him, the creative process was to a large extent completed before he put pen to paper. All witnesses of Mozart at work agree that he wrote a composition as one writes a

75

letter. He was in the habit of composing whole works in his mind and retaining them in his marvelous memory until he could no longer delay writing them out. His mind never really rested from music. As a critic has said, "Music was going on in his head continuously, probably in his sleep."

Mozart and his wife were always lacking money, and one of the "better" places they lived while in Vienna had a ceiling with attractive plaster ornamentation of sprites and cherubim. As Einstein observes, "I am convinced that Mozart never wasted a glance on it." Mozart said himself, "Composing is my one joy and passion." Composition with him was synonymous with life. He could always forget himself in composing. He was no lover of hunting and fishing, like his friend, Haydn, nor of communing with nature in the woods and fields, like Beethoven, Brahms, and Tchaikovsky. His joy was covering paper with music. Mozart never set out to be "original." He wrote music to please the public, though often his music is unique.

This supreme figure among the great composers of the world never had good health and his life was filled with difficulties, and yet these hardships rarely appeared in his music. Mozart's music is not autobiographical like that of Beethoven, for example. If Beethoven quarreled with a friend, you hear angry sounds in his music. Not so Mozart. He escaped into his music when the problems of life were the heaviest. In fact, his life was so full of cares that his music often has a carefree spirit.

Mozart's lively disposition, his love of fun, and the humanizing simplicity that he had which enabled him to carry gracefully his burden of genius came from his mother. His father, Leopold Mozart, was a composer of some ability, assistant director of the archbishop's chapel in Salzburg, and the author of a well-known book on violin playing. He probably would not be remembered today, other than for his violin treatise, and the *Toy* Symphony, if he had not been the father of Wolfgang Amadeus Mozart. But all the biographers agree that Mozart would not have achieved the character and the greatness he did without the influence of his father, who was an excellent teacher.

Mozart's musical education began when he was four years old along with his older sister, Maria Anna, or "Nannerl" as the family called her. Mozart seemed to know music innately. The main thing his father did was to guide and discipline the boy. At five, Mozart's international career began, and he was on tour over half of the time between the ages of five and 15. Most of his life he was very lively and had difficulty keeping still. He was often singing and jumping about, and amused at things other people scarcely noticed. His humor at times was bawdy. One can comprehend the playfulness of his nature by quoting a few words he wrote to "Nannerl" on one of the Italian tours. He was discussing a monk he had met in Bologna: "He is regarded as a holy man. For my part I do not believe it, for at breakfast he often takes a cup of chocolate and immediately afterwards a good glass of strong Spanish wine; and I myself have had the honor of lunching with this saint who at table drank a whole decanter and finished up with a full glass of strong wine, two large slices of melon, some peaches, pears, five cups of coffee, a whole plate of cloves, and two full saucers of milk and lemon. He may, of course, be following some sort of diet, but I do not think so, for it would be too much; moreover, he takes several little snacks during the afternoon . . ." (Einstein, *Mozart*).

Some critics say that Leopold was a calculating opportunist and exploited his children by taking them to the great European cities to play before the crowned heads and the aristocracy; but in the travels Mozart was brought in touch with every kind of music being written and heard in his day. The young Mozart absorbed with uncanny aptitude all that he heard. His music is a perfect blending of the Italian, German, and French styles. Broadly speaking, taste was the specialty of the Italian art, and knowledge of the German. The French contribution was elegance. Mozart, the Austrian, combined the three in his style.

His career as a composer began early. At six he wrote his first minuets. Shortly before his ninth birthday, he composed his first symphony. When he was 11, he wrote his first oratorio, and one year later he composed his first opera.

Another strong influence in his youth was the youngest son of J. S. Bach, Johann Christian Bach. They met in London in 1764, and it was Bach's son who first introduced him to the spirit of Italian music. Bach worshipped the Italian ideals of "beauty and form," and he gave time to the young Mozart, advising him, as well as listening to him, much to the boy's great pleasure.

Leopold saw to it that Mozart was steeped in every form of Italian music. The years 1770 to 1773 were largely occupied with traveling in Italy, studying, learning, observing, absorbing, and giving concerts. The importance of Mozart's Italian travels in his early teens cannot be overestimated. He spoke fluent Italian, and he was greatly helped by his counterpoint lessons which he had with Padre Martini in Bologna. He learned in Italy his unsurpassed ability to characterize life and humanity in music. Of all the major composers Mozart is the least locally rooted. Like Handel, he united the musical treasures of many nations.

The middle years of Mozart were given over to humiliating service for ungrateful patrons who treated the musicians in their court the same as any other servant. Often his pride was wounded by arrogant princes and archbishops, and Mozart truly hated them for their greed and failure to recognize his need. He longed for a sufficient income to allow him to be free, but never in his lifetime did he have it.

It is an irony difficult to comprehend: Mozart received little in payment for his colossal outpouring of beautiful music, and when he died, he was buried in a pauper's grave. To have any understanding of Mozart, however, we must accept the fact that he was a child and always remained one; and consequently, not only was he full of contradictions, but not at all practical or businesslike or orderly. Learning about great artists has been a special study of mine over the past 30 years and I have come to the conclusion that whether listening to Bach, Haydn, or Mozart, or looking at a Rembrandt etching or a Van Gogh or Pissarro painting, great art cannot be paid for. Today we have an opposite condition. Grants are given to those who call themselves composers, and yet their works prove that many of them have less talent than the cuckoo birds I heard this morning in the woods back of our chalet. Today in our museums we look at paintings which are not paintings, and yet the "artists" have received generous payment. It has been rightly said by a Rockford College professor who was speaking broadly about all the arts: "Never, in mankind's history, have stupidity and abomination been more generously rewarded with fame and money than they are in our time." I should like to say it again, rarely can great art be paid for.

From 1774 to 1781, Mozart lived chiefly in Salzburg, but as he traveled and saw other cities, he became more and more impatient with the provincial life of the town and the lack of musical opportunities. Seeking understanding and support for his career, he embarked on another long journey in 1777, this time with his mother, as he seemed incapable of taking care of himself. They finally went to Paris where every attempt at finding a good position or even appreciation ended in failure. When his mother died in Paris the following year, it was a terrible grief and shock to him. It cast him down and made him sad and discontent. It was a long time before he could even write to his father and tell what had happened. I will quote a brief portion of the letter. "I believe that no doctor, no man, no misfortune, no accident can give or take away a man's life, but only God." Finally he recovered his strength and went home.

Mozart may well be called the father of the modern concerto. He was the first to play a piano concerto in public and his improvisations were much admired. The piano was his favorite instrument, and he used it for some of his most personal expressions. Mozart believed that music should give delight to the one listening. Some critics consider his gentleness as weakness and think that his music is superficial. Pleasure is the most obvious reaction to his music. As has been said, he wrote a vast amount of music, and some of it, though delightful, can sound empty after a while. But there is always *another* Mozart composition one has never heard. A musician never outgrows the music of Mozart. He is the most sensitive of artists, and his taste is wonderful. He enjoyed sitting in a garden with the sound of birds around him while he composed, but more often he had to work without gardens and birds.

Song dominated his whole musical imagination after his travels in Italy, and it is true that Mozart makes the instruments sing. In writing his music he often used various colors of ink. The most difficult passages were in bright blue. The music of Mozart is clear, transparent, beautiful, and extremely difficult to perform.

Most of the works which make Mozart's name still famous were composed during his last ten years. This decade was fulfilling to him as an artist, yet heavy with disappointments and misery. After enduring more than his share of humiliating treatment, Mozart finally resigned his appointment by the archbishop of Salzburg and moved to other lodgings. The language of the archbishop upon hearing that Mozart had left the court is unprintable. Michael Haydn, the brother of Franz Joseph Haydn, also was in the

service of the archbishop and had been commissioned by
him to write six duets for violin and viola. He became ill
after writing four, and Mozart, who had a high opinion of
both brothers, came to the rescue with two duets in his
richest style. Michael Haydn submitted them with his own
and the archbishop showed no suspicion.

Against his father's will, Mozart married Constance
Weber in 1782, and thus began the "Pawnshop Period."
She was a poor and unsystematic housekeeper, somewhat
flighty, and his character faults and lack of tact did not add
to their fortune. From the day of his marriage until his
death, Mozart was always in difficulties for lack of money.
Leopold once said about his son, "With him there is either
too much or too little, never the golden mean. If he is not
actually in want, then he is immediately satisfied and becomes indolent and lazy. If he has to bestir himself, then
he realizes his worth and wants to make his fortune at
once."

The young couple moved 12 times in the next nine years
of their marriage; however, these moves were not as upsetting as one might think. The frequent changing of resi-
dence in Vienna gave the composer fresh stimulation.
Perhaps another reason they were always seeking a new
dwelling place was the fact that Mozart often spent half the
night at the pianoforte as these seemed to be his most
creative hours. It cannot be said too strongly: Mozart had a
phenomenal devotion to work, and yet he found time to
play billiards, go dancing, and to solve mathematical problems, another of his hobbies.

His life also continued to include traveling. Thus, to a
certain extent, one place suited him as well as another as
long as he was productive. He once wrote to his wife, "I
live quite retired here and don't go out the whole morning
but stick in my hole of a room and write." Whatever short-
comings the happy-go-lucky Constance had, Mozart loved
her dearly and wrote some of his best music after their
marriage.

In the same year he married Constance, Mozart met Franz Joseph Haydn. It was for each of them a stimulating and rewarding friendship. Instead of the jealousies and insincerities which often arise between talented people, the two musicians genuinely respected one another and learned from each other. The works of Haydn had a strong influence on Mozart's creativity as Haydn was more adventurous in his composing than Mozart. Both Haydn and Mozart wrote music either on commission or for a particular occasion. Their goal was that their music would be performed, that people would like it, and that they would make money from it. It worked for Haydn, because he had the protection of the Esterhazy princes for more than 30 years.

But despite his continuing reputation and the acclaim he enjoyed because of his operas Mozart was a free-lance composer and therefore did not benefit from the patronage of a genial archbishop or prince. And since there were no copyright laws in the 18th century, he lived all his life seeking financial security and never finding it. All that survive Mozart, besides his music and letters, are a few poor portraits, no two of which are alike. Most people fail to understand that creative works take a great deal of time to accomplish, and during those months or years the artist is earning nothing.

Mozart, in gratitude for all he had learned from his older friend, Franz Joseph Haydn, dedicated six string quartets to him. As we have said, song dominated Mozart's musical imagination after his visits to Italy, but Haydn revealed to him that instruments have "souls" too, and thus Mozart began to pour out an avalanche of instrumental compositions. The variety and richness of this music is beyond description. According to some critics, Mozart never surpassed the six *Haydn* quartets in his later works. Haydn, when he first heard the compositions, said to Mozart's father, "Before God and as an honest man I tell you that your son is the greatest composer known to me either in person or by name. He has taste, and what is more, the most profound knowledge of composition."

Mozart lived in the period known as "The Enlightenment." The complex movement began as a revolt of the spirit, a turning against supernatural religion and the church in favor of "natural" religion and practical morality. In the home of Leopold Mozart, religion held a prominent place. He was a devout and unquestioning Catholic. He was sure his son would emulate him, but these presumptions do not always follow. Towards the end of his life Mozart turned from formal religion to Freemasonry.

His last opera, *The Magic Flute* is a combination of morals and magic, Freemasonry and fairy tale. It is one of the greatest modern German operas, and is a testament to the brotherhood of man. Many of the ideas and rituals of Freemasonry go back to the period of cathedral building (900 to 1600). Today the Masons emphasize the fact that they do not foster any specific economic, political or religious creeds. They do spend millions of dollars for hospitals and homes for orphans, widows, and the aged, all of which is commendable, of course. But from a biblical point of view, they have turned aside from much of God's truth. Thus it is not clear if Mozart is writing the *Requiem* (his last composition) to the vague "great architect of the universe" (the Mason's terminology for the pantheistic god they affirm), or to the Lord of Lords and King of Kings.

Obviously we can discuss only a small part of Mozart's music in this brief study, but I should like to mention some of his compositions with which we all should be familiar. The *Prague* Symphony has been considered by various authorities as one of the most beautiful works in the history of music. The people of Prague were his truest and most consistent admirers and patrons. Mozart's Quintet for Clarinet and Strings in A is one of the most perfect works for the clarinet, and the graceful Serenade in G Major

(Eine Kleine Nachtmusik) is one of his most popular orchestral works.

In 1788, within a period of six weeks, Mozart composed his last three great symphonies. Symphony No. 39 in E Flat, Symphony No. 40 in G Minor, and the most famous, Symphony No. 41 in C Major, more popularly known as the *Jupiter* Symphony.

It is not only the amount of music that Mozart composed in his brief life that staggers the imagination—over 600 compositions under the Köchel listing—but the variety. His compositions include concertos, quartets, sonatas, divertimentos, serenades, and symphonies, and he is regarded as one of the greatest musical dramatists of all times. To do his operas justice would require many lectures. I will mention *The Marriage of Figaro,* as it set the model for all comic opera of the future. He made living characters for the first time in opera. Mozart's favorite form was opera, and he liked comic opera which expressed his own love of life. It is not astonishing that a mind as well-balanced as Mozart's should show so great a sense of humor. After his father died, and in a time of sorrow and decline, Mozart composed another of his masterpieces, the opera *Don Giovanni.*

Mozart lived in the period known also as the "Age of Elegance." Another name for 18th century music is Rococo, from a French word meaning shell. The time is characterized by an abundance of decorative scroll and shell work and by a general tendency towards elegance, hedonism, and frivolity. The emphasis on pleasantness and prettiness is in marked contrast to the impressive grandeur of the true Baroque style. Rococo elements are present in the works of both Haydn and Mozart.

As a musician I have been drawn to the music of Mozart most of my life. At seven I was enthusiastically conducting the G Minor Symphony in front of a victrola in my home in Virginia. During graduation services at Hollins College

I sang Mozart's beautiful "Psalm 117." Later I performed *Idomeneo* and the *Requiem Mass* with the Boston Symphony Orchestra. When auditioning for opera, I chose a Mozart aria; and at the dedication of the Flentrop organ in our L'Abri chapel, I had the joy of singing Mozart's "Alleluia" which he composed when he was 17 years old. I continue to sing the "Alleluia" with the L'Abri Ensemble.

Toward the end of Mozart's life, a mysterious visitor approached him and asked the sick and worn out composer to write a requiem for a certain nobleman and offered a good fee. The "mysterious visitor" was actually the servant of an eccentric nobleman who commissioned works and then had them performed as his own. Mozart accepted the commission, but he never finished it. He died when it was almost completed, believing even as he wrote it that it would be his own requiem. He did his last composing in bed. The opening theme of the "Kyrie" is one used by both Bach and Handel. This is not surprising. Mozart's encounter with the music of J. S. Bach earlier in his life had caused a crisis in his creativity, and the impact of what he had learned from Bach was deep and lasting.

In one of the last letters Mozart wrote to his father he said, "I never lie down at night without reflecting that, young as I am, I may not live to see another day. Yet no one of all my acquaintances could say that in company I am morose or disgruntled. For this blessing I daily thank my Creator."

Mozart died in misery 5 December 1791, and his body was taken to a pauper's tomb. When the hearse approached the cemetery, a thunderstorm broke and no one followed the coffin to the unmarked grave. Yet the sheer beauty, perfection, and profundity of his music continues to astonish and delight the world through the years. Great music is costly, not to those of us who listen, but to those who make it.

Recommended Reading

Davenport, Marcia. *Mozart*. New York: Charles Scribners
and Sons, 1932.

Einstein, Alfred. *Mozart: His Character, His Work*. London: Oxford University Press, 1945.

Recommended Listening

Ave, Verum Corpus
Concerto for Flute and Harp
Concerto for Piano—C Minor
Don Giovanni
Exsultate, Jubilate
The Magic Flute
The Marriage of Figaro
Hayden Quartets
Serenade *Eine Kleine Nachtmusic*
Quintet in A for Clarinet
Sonata No. 8 for Piano
Symphony 35, *Haffner*
Symphony No. 39
Symphony No. 38
Symphony No. 40 G Minor
Symphony No. 41, *Jupiter*

Chapter VII

Ludwig van Beethoven
(1770—1827)

"The genius who was before all others a law unto himself."—Marek

The concept that what a man believes effects his work is clearly exemplified in the life and music of that colossal figure in history, Ludwig van Beethoven. His motto was "Freedom above all." He became a legend in his own lifetime, and his figure overshadows the whole of 19th century music. The slogan of Jean Jacques Rousseau, "Myself alone," became the rallying cry of all the new movements in writing, painting, and music. Neither Goethe nor Beethoven is imaginable without Voltaire, Rousseau, or the early Romantics. Soon Beethoven became the propulsive force and the idol of the Romantics. With "heroic man" at the center of the universe, humanism reached a pinnacle in the age of Beethoven and Goethe.

Beethoven almost worshiped Goethe, Germany's most famous writer. Like the literary genius, Beethoven believed that it is the artist's task to express both the turmoil and the peace within oneself, and to search for one's own perfection. Beethoven's music is full of violent contrast. Renoir, the French painter, observed that Beethoven is "positively indecent the way he tells us about himself; he doesn't spare us either the pain in his heart or the pain in his stomach." The music of Beethoven has a frenzied, "demonic" energy. It is volcanic and exuberant and suddenly melts into tenderness and sadness, then again bursts into fury. It is a direct outpouring of his personality.

Beethoven was one of the great thinkers in the realm of music. Early he got rid of the frivolous. His intellectual curiosity was enormous, and he continued to learn all his life. If only subconsciously, he merged the two concepts of the Enlightenment and the Romantic movements, the clear resoluteness of the one, and the dark introspection of the other. Both are present in his music. This gigantic individualist, a born antagonist, was set on conquering. Profoundly convinced of the dignity of man, Beethoven believed fanatically in freedom without limits. Romain Rolland has said, "There is something in him of Nietzsche's superman, long before Nietzsche."

Ludwig van Beethoven was born in Bonn, Germany, in 1770. He began studying music at the age of four, but under traumatic conditions. His father and a musician friend would return home late at night after visiting the taverns. They would awaken the boy and force him to have a music lesson until the early morning hours. Drinking was an accepted feature of the Beethoven household. His grandmother was also an alcoholic.

The young Beethoven was unmethodical, and even as a child, he was a prey to melancholy. But he had tremendous musical ambition and physical strength. While still very young, he was employed as an organist, though he later gained fame as a piano virtuoso. In 1787 in Vienna he met and played for Mozart who prophesied a bright future for him. While there he was called back to Bonn by the disturbing news of his mother's failing health. She died of consumption at the age of 40 not too long after he returned home. She was a good, kind person, and Beethoven loved her. His loss brought on the first of those emotional crises that recurred throughout his life. He never abandoned the search for a woman like his mother, and he never found her. There were many women in Beethoven's life, especially among the nobility. As one historian said, "Beethoven was always in love." He considered marriage a few times, but for various reasons he remained a bachelor.

Five long years after his first visit to Vienna, Beethoven set out again for this city, one of the centers of the musical world. By now Mozart was lying in an unmarked pauper's grave. The French Revolution was soon to enter its most terrible stage, The Reign of Terror. Goethe was in Weimar directing the ducal theatre, and Haydn was enjoying fame throughout Europe.

Beethoven had some lessons with Haydn in Vienna, and he dug deep into his studies though in his opinion Haydn was a poor teacher. Undoubtedly Haydn was too busy to concentrate on teaching, but he did something better for the young, unknown musician. He sent several of Beethoven's compositions to the Elector of Cologne and recommended that he receive money to continue his career as a composer.

Beethoven learned to compose like his predecessors before he found his own style. He never, like many 20th-century composers, cut himself off from the past. As a boy he had mastered Bach's *The Well-tempered Clavier,* and he had a lifelong veneration for the music of Handel and Mozart. Once he said, "Handel is the greatest, the most able of all composers. I can still learn from him." And Beethoven was still learning from Handel the year before he died. Always a student, he was of all composers the least inclined to repeat himself. A friend wondered why he did not have Handel's works. Beethoven replied, "How

should I, a poor devil, have got them?" It took his friend
two years, but he made a secret vow to send Handel's
music to him, everything he could find. In December,
1826, a fine edition of Handel in 40 volumes arrived.
While he was lying ill the last few months of his life, Beethoven used to lean the books against the wall, turn pages
and break into exclamations of joy and praise as he studied
Handel.

Sir Julius Benedict described his first sight of Beethoven: "He was a short, stout man with a very red face, small
piercing eyes, and bushy eyebrows, dressed in a very long
overcoat which reached nearly to his ankles." He also had
long white hair which touched his broad shoulders.

Beethoven saw himself as a creator "set apart" from
ordinary people. Anything or anyone who interferred with
his creativity he brushed aside. He could be up in arms at
the most trifling fancied slight to himself. He was full of
scorn for nearly everyone: the poor, the aristocracy, those
who admired him, those who hated him, common people,
the weak and feeble. As Marek says, "The mystery of a
complex personality can never be wholly unraveled, and
surely not that of a man as complex as Beethoven."

In Vienna, Beethoven moved in the circle of the nobility, and a long line of influential people helped his career
in spite of his outbursts of arrogance and blistering rude-
ness. At the outset of his career, Beethoven was a virtuoso
pianist. In the Second Piano Concerto, the earliest orchestral score he saw fit to publish, the last movement has a
haunting flavor reminiscent of Mozart and Haydn.

From time to time Beethoven had a few pupils, but he
must have been one of the most unsystematic teachers the
world has known, being impatient, slovenly, quarrelsome,
unbelievably sensitive, and never on time. That marvelous
organizer of music was the most disorganized of persons. I
mentioned that Mozart and his wife changed their resi-
dence 12 times in 9 years; Beethoven, in 35 years in Vien-

na, moved at least 70 times. In the many paintings of the great composer, there is often a grand piano. I wonder how many stairs it was carried up and down in these frequent changes of address.

Always an early riser (5 or 6 A.M.), Beethoven liked to work in the morning and had the habit of composing out-of-doors while taking long walks. He said, "I love a tree more than a man." Beethoven loved the natural world, but as a pantheist who worships nature rather than the Creator. "Beethoven was not the man to bow to anyone—even God!" said David Ewen. Basically Rousseau's idea was that the creative person should not be at home in society, but seek solitude "to express oneself, one's feelings," and to delve into the unconscious, to uncover the mystery in one's inner self. On one occasion a friend made for Beethoven a copy of one of his scores. He signed it, "With God's help." Underneath it Beethoven scrawled, "O man, help yourself."

Beethoven rarely had to write music at anyone's command and could afford to "think and think" and revise until it suited him, as he had no deadlines to meet. But he wrote his music with great difficulty, and he subjected himself to severe criticism. He began to keep notebooks as a youth, and his notebooks are crowded with a welter of musical ideas in all stages of development which make them comparable to those of Leonardo da Vinci. He felt a titantic force of creation within himself. Beethoven's life was one of incessant creativity.

Beethoven's increasing deafness, which began as early as 1798 when he was only 28, forced him to abandon his career as a virtuoso and to use his energy for composition. The first symptoms of his impending deafness must have puzzled and frightened him. He tried various doctors and cures and grew increasingly distrustful of everyone. As his biographer Marek shows, Beethoven wrote to a friend, "My poor hearing haunted me everywhere like a ghost;

and I avoided . . . all human society." At one period he was
tempted to commit suicide, "But only Art held me back,"
he explained, "for it seemed unthinkable for me to leave
the world before I had produced all that I felt called upon
to produce." A little later when he began to take courage
again, he uttered the famous words, "I will seize Fate by
the throat." He flung out the challenge to himself and a
parade of Romantic artists after him. "It shall certainly not
bend and crush me completely," he said.

In the years roughly between 1802 and 1816, Beethoven had a prodigious outpouring of creativity. His courage
was not steadfast. There were black times, but in those 14
years he composed six symphonies, the *Coriolan* Overture,
Fidelio, the last two piano concertos, the middle quartets,
and piano sonatas through Op. 90, including the *Appassionata.*

In 1816 he was appointed guardian to his nephew, Karl.
Even though he loved the boy in his commanding, tem-
peramental way, Karl was a source of constant trouble to
Beethoven the rest of his life. At one time Karl attempted
to kill himself. Finally they quarreled more violently than
all the other times and Beethoven never saw his nephew
again.

By 1817 his hearing was completely gone, but it is prob-
able that Beethoven could "hear" music by feeling the
vibrations. The burden of his deafness helped to bring to
focus what was to become one of the themes of the 19th
century—the loneliness of man.

When Beethoven conducted the first performance of his
Ninth Symphony, because of his deafness he could not
hear the applause and someone had to turn him around so
he could see the enthusiasm of the audience. As his
creativity increased, he withdrew more and more, even
from friends, and although his fame had spread over
Europe, Beethoven lived almost as a recluse.

Historically Beethoven's work was built on the

achievements of the Classical Period, but his figure towers like a colossus astride the 18th and 19th centuries, like a bridge to Romanticism. He is the last in the triad of Viennese classics—Haydn, Mozart, and Beethoven. Before Beethoven, musicians had been creators in an ordered universe. Beethoven wrestled with destiny, and his music became a means of expressing his ideas about humanity. Some critics have referred to him as the prophet of self-will, and his weakness was his pride.

It is generally agreed that the music of Beethoven may be divided into three periods: Imitation, Externalization and Reflection. The first period, Imitation, goes to about 1802 and includes the six quartets, Op. 18, the first 10 piano sonatas, the first two symphonies, and two piano concertos. The period of Externalization runs roughly between 1802 and 1816. As mentioned before these were years of great creativity. In the final period, Reflection, extending from 1817 till his death, Beethoven wrote the *Missa Solemnis in D,* the Ninth Symphony, the last piano sonatas, and the last five quartets.

The piano occupied a central position in Beethoven's art. He wrote 32 piano sonatas which are to piano literature what the plays of Shakespeare are to the drama. For Beethoven the piano sonata was the vehicle for his boldest and most inward thoughts.

Concerto No. 5 (*The Emperor*) was written while Napoleon's guns were hammering at the gates of Vienna. It was reported that Beethoven took refuge in a cellar with his head thrust into a pillow to help save the remnant of his hearing.

One of the main features of Beethoven's music is the profoundness of emotional content. In the *Appassionata* Beethoven came to the full realization that the piano is a percussion instrument. It ends in an orgy of musical fist shaking. Characteristic are the violent contrasts between pianissimo and fortissimo. Until Beethoven's era, most music held a measure of predictability. One of Beethoven's outstanding characteristics is the element of surprise—his unpredictability.

Beethoven wrote 10 violin sonatas, the most famous being the *Kreutzer* Sonata. Here the violin has percussive declamations. It is even more celebrated because Tolstoy wrote a novel called *The Kreutzer Sonata* about a jealous husband who murders his wife.

His one opera, *Fidelio,* which is among the greatest, gave him more trouble than any of his other works. Beethoven was a superb dramatic musician, but he rarely wrote well for voices. He disregarded the limitations of the human voice and considered it just another instrument. He is frequently unvocal.

It is impossible to discuss Beethoven's symphonies with adequacy in a few words. Each of them possesses a complete and separate individuality, but we will briefly comment on each one.

The First Symphony is the most Classical of the nine symphonies.

The Second Symphony was written during the time he began to realize he was becoming deaf. He wrote it in intervals between black depression. It has a simplicity and a sunshine radiance full of energy and fire.

The Third Symphony stands as an immortal expression of heroic greatness. It is a work of nobility and grandeur. Beethoven dedicated it to Napoleon whom he idealized as a hero leading humanity to a new age of liberty, equality, and fraternity. But when Beethoven heard that Napoleon had crowned himself Emperor, he angrily tore up the dedication page and renamed the symphony the *Eroica*.

Musically the age of Napoleon (1769-1821) is the age of Beethoven. The age of Revolution took place during the great awakening of the human ego in philosophy and in art. The philosophers of the 18th century Enlightenment prepared the way for the political explosion that is called the age of Revolution. The symbol of the Enlightenment was a question mark, and the star of the Enlightenment was Voltaire, one of the greatest of all French writers, who questioned the reliability of the Bible and placed his confidence in man's reason. Voltaire's enemy was Rousseau who had little faith in reason. He believed in action, freedom, and the goodness of humanity, but his own character and life were something else. His mistress had five children and Rousseau sent them all to orphanages.

The Fourth Symphony is full of energy. In it Beethoven releases tumults of exultant strength.

The Fifth Symphony is a musical depiction of Beethoven's struggle with deafness. Like Goethe, Beethoven believed in a pitiless fate.

The Sixth or *Pastoral* Symphony is the starting point of Romantic music. It is the only symphony to which Beethoven gave a program. Each of the five movements suggests a scene from life in the country. Beethoven told a friend that the quail, cuckoos, nightingales, and yellow hammers around Heiligenstadt, where he spent several summers, had helped him compose the Sixth Symphony.

The Seventh Symphony contains one of the most famous of Beethoven's movements, the Second, which, perhaps has had the most influence on the Romantic composers. The whole symphony is controlled by persistent rhythmic ideas. Wagner called it the "apotheosis of the dance."

The Eighth Symphony is urbane and sophisticated.

The Ninth Symphony is a paean to the universal brotherhood of man, and in it he asserts the arrival of joy through suffering. The most striking novelty of the symphony is the use of chorus and solo voices as if the orchestra had developed to such an advanced stage it could go no further and needed the collaboration of the vocal art.

The last five quartets of Beethoven together with the

Great Fugue are regarded as the summit of his achievement. As Burk says, "The last five quartets can be looked
upon as the crown of all that he did, and all that had gone
before as a preparation." These occupied him almost exclusively in the last three years of his life. The tortured,
unyielding spirit of Beethoven needed isolation to work,
and the five quartets express his unutterable loneliness and
alienation as he shut himself off from everyone. Music, for
Beethoven, became a matter of withdrawal.

Those of us who live in a century following an artist of
such extraordinary talent and supreme dedication as Beethoven cannot escape his influence. Grout says, "Beethoven was the most powerful disruptive force in the history
of music. His works opened the gateway to a new world."
And, may I add, to a disintegrating world. By saying this,
we do not mean his music is not beautiful, amazing, noble,
and sublime. God is the giver of gifts, but not all gifted
persons acknowledge and give thanks to God.

Recently I was asked by a student at L'Abri, "What does
philosophy have to do with music?" One of the aims of this
book is to show how our thought world effects what we do
in life. The fact that Beethoven held a world view that
excluded spiritual wholeness caused his music to move in a
direction of disintegration toward the end of his life.

As a composer his was one endless quest for the ideal
form that would completely express the unity he had en-
visioned from the beginning, but as Francis Schaeffer has
explained in his book *How Should We Then Live?*
humanism fails to bring unity and does not answer life's
crucial questions. The revealed biblical truth of the Triune
God offers the only world view that provides a unity between universal absolutes and the particulars of human
existence. In Jesus Christ, God offers an individual believer a spiritual wholeness and intellectual satisfaction
that give meaning and content to life.

Beethoven's last quartets, being consistent with his
world view, turn to the abstract and mystical. "The late

Beethoven," according to Einstein, "has been considered a destroyer of form." The language of the last quartets is austere and the structure unpredictable. Some movements are unusually long, others astonishingly short. The frequent dissonances anticipate 20th-century music. As the music of Beethoven became more mystical, it moved towards the complete dissolution of traditional forms. Another feature of his late work is the continuity he achieved by intentionally blurring dividing lines. One senses the beginning of the loss of categories.

In these quartets Beethoven used fragmentary thematic materials and vague tonalities. In fact, the formal use of thematic material was abandoned and, instead, theme breaks in upon theme. The fragments of melody are varied, transformed, then almost wilfully interrupted and recalled. This principle of variation is later picked up and carried much further by Arnold Schönberg in his perpetual variations, about which we will be speaking in another chapter.

Beethoven's last quartets have been called the music of the future, and much of what we are listening to today has come as a result of Beethoven's influence.

Beethoven was born a Catholic, but he never attended church. On his deathbed (he died of pneumonia complicated by cirrhosis of the liver and dropsy), he did take the last sacrament, but he viewed all priests with mistrust. Marek describes Beethoven's death: "The day was very cold; snow had fallen. Around five o'clock a sudden thunderstorm obscured the sky. It became very dark. Suddenly, there was a great flash of lightning which illuminated the death chamber, accompanied by violent claps of thunder. At the flash of lightning, Beethoven opened his eyes, raised his tightly clenched right hand, and fell back dead. It was about 5:15 P.M., March 26, 1827." Huge crowds attended his funeral. Franz Schubert was one of the torchbearers.

People all over the world know and appreciate the music

of Beethoven. In one sense, his music appeals to us because much of it expresses his struggle and suffering, and we identify with him. Often in his letters Beethoven asked the question, "What is the use of it all?" But when composing he rarely asked the question until the latter part of his life. In much of his music Beethoven balanced suffering with solace which gave the impression of strength.

By all means, we should listen to the music of Beethoven. His music brings together thoughts and emotions which often are more intense than we can produce. But never listen indifferently and without discernment. Enjoy and appreciate that which is good, but hold in mind that it is with composers as it is with all of us: What we believe effects our total life.

Recommended Reading

Burk, John N. *The Life and Work of Beethoven.* New York: Randon House (Modern Library), 1943.

Landon, H. C. Robbins, ed. *Beethoven: A Documentary Study.* London: Thames and Hudson, 1974.

Marek, George R. *Beethoven: Biography of a Genius.* New York: Thomas Y. Crowell, 1969.

Recommended Listening

Five Piano Concertos
Concerto in D for Violin
Fidelio
Last Five Quartets
Piano Sonata No. 8 *Pathetique*
Piano Sonata No 14 *Moonlight*
Piano Sonata No. 21 *Waldstein*
Piano Sonata No. 23 *Appassionata*
Violin Sonata No. 9 *Kreutzer*
All nine symphonies

Chapter VIII
Franz Schubert
(1797—1828)

"Nor is that musician most praiseworthy who hath longest played, but he in measured accents who hath made sweetest melody."—William Drummond

The early teachers of Schubert watched him in silent astonishment at the rapidity with which he absorbed instruction. Holzer (one of his first teachers) said, "The lad has harmony in his little finger." Later at the choir school of the Royal Chapel, Ruziczka, court organist, teacher, and conductor of the orchestra, in an attempt to explain Schubert's swiftness to learn, exclaimed, "He has learned it from God."

The musical education of Schubert actually began at home. Schubert's father was an amateur cellist, and he was the boy's first music teacher. Between the merciless grind of teaching and the implacable routine of raising and burying children (of 14, 9 died in infancy) the parish schoolmaster encouraged and cultivated music in his home. Schubert's father taught him to play the violin, and his older brother, Ignaz, gave him his first piano lessons. They soon recognized their inadequacy as teachers, and at the age of seven, Schubert was apprenticed to the choirmaster of the parish church, Michael Holzer.

During his holidays from the choir school, Schubert formed a family string quartet trying out his music. Another brother, Ferdinand, who remained close to Schubert all his life, once said that the family rehearsals were frequently interrupted by the young composer correcting the faults of the father with a gentle, "Sir! there must be a mistake somewhere."

Early in life Schubert learned to live with hardships. At the Imperial and Royal Seminary the music room was left unheated, even in the winter. But in spite of that, there was plenty of music. The school orchestra performed an entire symphony every evening and finished off with the "noisiest possible overture." In warm weather the school windows were left open, and people crowded around to listen to the free concerts until the police complained that the gatherings obstructed traffic and finally dispersed the crowd.

At one concert, Joseph von Spaun, who was a student of law and nine years older than Schubert, turned around to see who was behind him playing the violin so well. He discovered a very small boy in spectacles. Later in one of the practice rooms Schubert played a Mozart sonata for him, and urged on by Spaun, the shy and blushing Schubert played a minuet of his own composition. He told his new friend that he "sometimes put his thoughts into notes," but very secretly, so his father would not think he was neglecting his studies. Schubert began composing when only 13 years old, and he wrote his first song the next year. He began his first symphony in 1813.

In his choir school days, Schubert impressed everyone with his musical gifts, but they were also aware of his moral qualities. Because of his reliability, Schubert was privileged to leave the school and to have special lessons with Salieri, who had been a friend of Haydn and was one of Beethoven's teachers. As Grout summarizes it: "Schubert's training in music theory was not systematic, but his environment, both at home and in school was saturated with music-making."

The cheerful amateur activities at the choir school and the pleasure he received singing in the church choir, sometimes as the soloist, were the positive side of his schooling, but the negative aspect sounds familiar when studying the lives of famous composers. Poverty, particularly in early life, seems to be the conventional requirement for the development of a composer, coupled with unending determination to overcome impossible circumstances. Most of his life Schubert was so poor he could not afford to buy paper on which to write his music, and he rarely had his own piano.

Schubert seldom had enough to eat at the choir school. In a letter to his brother, Ferdinand, the youthful Schubert wrote, "You will know from your own experience that there are times when one could certainly do with a roll and a few apples, particularly when one has to wait eight and a half hours between a moderate-sized mid-day meal and a wretched sort of supper. . . . How would it be, then, if you were to let me have a few *kreuzer* each month? You wouldn't notice them, and they would make me happy and contented in my cell. . . . I rely on the words of the Apostle Matthew, especially where he says: Let him who hath two coats, give one to the poor.

> Your affectionate, poor, hopeful and once again *poor* brother,
> Franz"*

*Franz Schubert's Letters, edited by O. E. Deutsch (New York: Vienna House, 1974), p. 23

Even though one might question the accuracy of the biblical quotation, the letters of Schubert are as delightful to read as his music is to listen to. In fact, they are a counterpart of his music: The style is simple, melodic, and diatonic. Schubert, whether in words or music, expresses in the most direct way the fundamentals of things without self-consciousness or the desire to produce a large dramatic effect. Schubert in another letter to Ferdinand, this time concerning his music, said, "What I feel in my heart I give to the world." Schubert's letters, especially in the earlier period, show the contrast of joy and sadness so characteristic in his music.

Franz Peter Schubert was born in 1797 in Vienna. He was the youngest in the family. His father was a God-fearing, strict, but kindly and honorable schoolmaster. Schubert's mother, like Haydn's, was a professional cook. Also like Haydn, and several other composers, Schubert was selected to be a Vienna choirboy because of his beautiful soprano voice. Even though his heart was elsewhere, he was educated to be a school teacher. His father did not consider composing music a profession, but there was no way to stop the melodies from filling his mind. His art was his life, and his life was his art.

He taught for three miserable years, then in 1816 his friend, Schober, a restless poet, offered him a place to live and opened the door to the freedom so necessary for his creativity. However, even the frustration of teaching school had not stopped his composing, but it had been a physical and emotional strain for him. Schubert was only five feet one and a half inches tall. He had a warm, gentle, friendly, profoundly simple personality, but he was extremely modest, and with his head spinning with music, he could not help being an indifferent teacher.

Shortly before he was freed from teaching, he was in his room reading Goethe's poem, *The Erlking*. His friend, Spaun, passed by to see the young composer and found him in a state of high excitement. Even as he was reading he could hear the music in his head and was reciting the poem and hurling notes on a piece of music-paper at the same time. Within less than an hour his composition was finished. Some critics consider "The Erlking" the greatest of all lieder. The accompaniment of "The Erlking" is very effective. Schubert brings the piano into equality with the voice. It is the closest that music has ever come to a complete union with poetry. Schubert was to the song what Beethoven was to the symphony, Wagner to the music drama, and Chopin to the piano.

Of the eight great composers of the 18th and 19th centuries whose names are closely associated with Vienna, Gluck, Haydn, Mozart, Beethoven, Schubert, Bruckner, Brahms, and Mahler, only Franz Schubert was actually born there. Schubert rarely left Vienna except for a few excursions with friends and two summers spent in Hungary as a music teacher to the two daughters of Count Johann Esterhazy. At first he was in high spirits in Hungary, but soon he missed the stimulation of his artistic friends. He wrote in a letter to one of them, "Not a soul here has any feeling for true art . . . so I am alone with my beloved [muse], and have to hide her in my room, in my piano, and in my heart. . . . It is fairly quiet, except for 40 geese which sometimes set up such a cackling that one cannot hear oneself speak" (Flower, *Schubert*). Even though the Esterhazy interludes were not really to his liking, nothing was wasted as far as his music was concerned. Schubert was much influenced by Hungarian and gypsy music.

It is impossible to discuss the life and music of Schubert separately, because they are one. If he was not composing, he was thinking, talking, playing, or listening to music. He was overjoyed when beautiful music was performed. His friends, and he had many who later went on to make names for themselves in the different arts and professions, spoke of his natural simplicity, his frank, open, sunny disposition, and generous nature. Flower tells that according to one friend, "His was a magnificent soul. I never saw him jealous or grudging of others; the childlikeness of his mind and the lack of guile, are beyond expression."

Schubert never married, and for him friendship was the joy of his life. After giving up teaching Schubert was penniless, but his friends came to his aid. Schober provided lodging, someone else found him appliances, they took their meals together, and the person who had any money paid the bill. Schubert was the leader of the party and he was known by several affectionate nicknames. Among his friends, besides Spaun and Schober, were the poets, Grillparzer and Mayrhofer, the singer, Vogl, painters, Schwind and Kupelweiser, Dietrich, the sculptor, and Franz Lachner, afterwards the court *Kapellmeister* to the King of Bavaria. These friends not only bought paper on which he could write his music, but they organized periodical meetings which they called "Schubert Tiaden." Other friends and influential people were invited to these musical evenings to hear Schubert's compositions. His songs were usually sung by Vogl with Schubert at the piano. Vogl, a well-known Viennese singer who especially appreciated the Bible, showed unusual kindness to the sensitive Schubert. Schwind's drawing of a Schubertian evening is well known. These meetings were not only social occasions: Besides the music of Schubert's inexhaustible pen, poems were read and drawings and sketches were discussed.

If Schubert had not had his friends, it is possible we would not have his music. They were the ones who listened to it, enjoyed it, and gave him the encouragement to go write more. After his brief teaching career he spent the rest of his short life doing more or less what he wanted. But he was never lazy nor dissipated. He had a weakness for wine, but his indulgences were brief and he always came back to his work. Often at night he would meet some of his friends in a favorite restaurant for music, talk, food and drink, but nearly always Schubert would leave before the others. He composed both carefully and ceaselessly. When someone asked, "How do you compose?" he answered, "When I have finished one piece, I begin another." Daily Schubert studied and composed six or seven hours, a methodical habit he learned from his father.

Apart from his friends and close surroundings, Schubert never was a success in his lifetime, but posterity has caused his music to become a lasting international treasure. He is the classical example of a composer, artist, or writer so devoted to his art that he never manages to live well or come to terms with publishers and the world. His pitifully brief life illustrates the tragedy of genius overwhelmed by the necessities and annoyances of daily living. But Schubert, with the exception of his years in the choir school, rarely went hungry. He could always sell a song for the price of a meal, and often he did.

Schubert is known as the musicians' musician. Liszt called him "the most poetic musician who ever lived." As Ernest Newman says, "The simplicities of a Schubert or a Mozart may go deeper than the sophistications of many a more intellectual composer."

The contemporaries of Schubert had no idea of his significance. The music critics today speak of Franz Schubert as the greatest writer of songs and one of the supreme creators of melody. It is an overwhelming statement when we consider the multitude of songs that have been composed in the past and are being written today. Like many gifted persons, he wrote too many songs, but his best are the best. In his short life of 31 years he wrote an enormous amount of music besides his songs. Schubert followed unreservedly a single impulse—to create.

Schubert can be compared to the great English Romantic poet, John Keats, who died at 26. Those who composed in the Romantic period had a strong literary orientation, and the one main characteristic Romantic form was the lied (or song) with its dependence on poetry.

As Schubert wrote more than 600 lieder, only a few numbers can be mentioned. The "Ave Maria" with words by Sir Walter Scott is a good example of a song dependent on poetry. Its simple greatness and magical effect of harmonic shifts is typical of Schubert. "An die Musik" with words by his friend, Schober, is another exquisite song. One phrase, "To music which leads to a better world," could be regarded as the motto for all of Schubert's music. Also to be cited among the great poetic songs are "Gretchen at the Spinning Wheel," with words by Goethe, and "Hark, Hark the Lark" and "Who is Sylvia?", both with words by Shakespeare.

Some critics speak of Schubert as a dreamer who lived a disorganized and easygoing life. It is not true. Even while walking about seemingly doing nothing, he was searching for inspiration. At times Schubert suffered terrible headaches and periods of depression, and the walks undoubtedly helped to relieve him.

The story of how Schubert composed "Hark, Hark the Lark" probably was repeated more than once in his life. According to the well known story Schubert was walking past an outdoor café when he saw some friends at one of the tables. He joined them and picked up from the table a volume of Shakespeare which one of the friends had been reading outloud. Glancing idly through the pages as the others talked, his eye caught the lines of "Hark, Hark the Lark." Immediately his face was aglow. "Such a lovely melody has come into my head," he said. "If only I had some paper!" One friend quickly drew lines across the back of a menu, and Schubert scribbled down the notes as fast as he could. Later he took home his song and the Shakespeare book, and that same evening composed "Who is Sylvia?" Thus two beautiful songs were born.

The works of Schubert also include overtures, dances, chamber music, operas, sonatas and symphonies. One of the most delightful compositions Schubert wrote was the Quintet in A, or *The Trout.* It gets its name from the third movement which is based on a Schubert song. A wealthy cellist who held musical evenings in Vogl's home asked Schubert to contribute a new work, and so he wrote the Quintet. As Schubert often wrote specifically for the musicians at hand, the Quintet has a very exciting part for a double bass. The piece is full of musical charm and the magical Schubertian modulations. Schubert most always wrote at headlong speed, and much of his work is fresh, vivid, spontaneous, and bearing the mark of improvisation.

By the age of 21 Schubert had already written six symphonies. The two-movement Symphony No. 8 in B Minor, more well known as the *Unfinished* Symphony, can be called the first truly Romantic symphony. Schubert's inspiration had its roots in Beethoven. He complained to a friend one day, "Who can do anything after Beethoven?" Having said that, he still had the courage to write his symphony. It really is not unfinished as in it Schubert said everything he had to say on the theme of melancholy. It was first performed 35 years after his death, and today the Unfinished Symphony ranks with the finest of Beethoven. Schubert should encourage each one of us to make our statement. It might be better than we think.

Schubert worshipped Beethoven from afar, and even though they often ate in the same restaurant, the modest Schubert never approached his hero. When Beethoven was on his deathbed, Schubert was one of the few people he asked to see in his last days, because shortly before his fatal illness, Beethoven had seen about 60 of Schubert's songs. He said several times, "Truly this Schubert has the divine fire."

In 1828 Schubert wrote his Ninth Symphony in C Major. It is the last mighty Classical symphony. Though the music of Schubert is Romantic in its lyrical quality and harmonic color, nevertheless he always maintained a certain Classical serenity and poise. The symphony was refused performance because it was considered "too long and too difficult."

Robert Schumann when he was in Vienna, not only visited the grave of Schubert, but also his brother, Ferdinand. There he discovered the Ninth Symphony among "a fabulous pile" of manuscripts.

Schubert's music always sounds good. The beauty of sound was essential to him. He learned to write for orchestras by playing in an orchestra. He had the power of making instruments sing. His ideal composer was Mozart, and the last months of his life he was studying Handel. One time after hearing some music by Mozart, Schubert wrote in a letter, "Happy moments relieve the sadness of life. Up in heaven these radiant moments will turn into joy perpetual."*

During his latter years, Schubert took a renewed interest in church music which had always stirred him deeply. Franz Schubert was a man who accepted religious principles and strict dogma. In spite of the struggles of his life his faith remained unshaken, and was adorned by some of his richest compositions.

At the end of his life, Schubert wrote the song cycle *Die Winterreise* which includes some of the best songs ever written, yet Schubert was forced to sell them for almost nothing because of his grievous financial state. He said that these songs affected him more deeply than any of his other songs. Here he expressed the extremes of pathos. Schubert did have times when he was obsessed by the seeming failure of his life. But even in the tragic music of the final years, there is no bitterness, only a darkening of the wist-

---

Franz Schubert's Letters, edited by O. E. Deutsch (New York: Vienna House, 1974), p. 32

fulness that makes much of his music so poignant. Schubert died at 31 of typhoid fever, and his request to be buried next to Beethoven was fulfilled.

From Bauernfeld's *Diary* (one of Schubert's many friends):

20 Nov. 1828

"Yesterday afternoon Schubert died. On Monday I still spoke with him. On Tuesday he was delirious, on Wednesday dead. To the last he talked to me of our opera. It all seems like a dream to me. The most honest soul and the most faithful friend! I wish I lay there in his place. For he leaves the world with fame!"

Recommended Reading

Deutsch, Otto Erich. *The Schubert Reader. A Life of Franz Schubert in Letters and Documents.* New York: W. W. Norton, 1947.

Flower, Newman. *Franz Schubert: The Man and His Circle.* New York: Tudor Publishing Co., 1935.

Hutchings, Arthur. *Schubert.* London: J. M. Dent, 1967.

Recommended Listening

Impromptus
Quartet in D minor *Death and the Maiden*
Quintet in A, *The Trout*
Rosamunde—Incidental music
Any of his songs
Die Schöne Müllerin
Die Winterreise
Symphony No. 8, *Unfinished*
Symphony No. 9, *The Great*
Wanderer Fantasie for Piano

Chapter IX

Felix Mendelssohn

(1809—1847)

"It is a relief to find one musician who was really happy for the greater part of his life, even though that life was a short one."—Siegmund Spaeth

At the age of 17 Mendelssohn composed the enchanting overture to Shakespeare's *A Midsummer-Nights's Dream.* He never surpassed this music, and it set the standard for all subsequent concert overtures of the Romantic period. It was first performed in 1826 in the family garden house with a private orchestra under Mendelssohn's direction. Its sparkling melodies and brilliant orchestration established the young Mendelssohn as one of the leading composers of his day. Seventeen years later he added about a dozen pieces making this programmatic orchestral suite.

He made his first public appearance as a pianist when nine years old, and he began to write music when he was 10. His first teacher was his mother, a lady of exceptional culture and refinement. In Berlin where the family moved in 1812, Mendelssohn studied with Carl Zelter and other excellent teachers who introduced the boy to the finest music. Zelter, for all his gruffness and severity, regarded his young pupil with great pride and affection. In fact, Zelter was so impressed with his 11-year-old pupil, he took him to Weimar to visit Goethe. The famous poet-philosopher accepted the precocious boy on terms of equality, and the young Mendelssohn and the 72-year-old writer became close friends.

The prospect of their son visiting Goethe threw the Mendelssohn family into great excitement. His sister, Fanny, wrote to him: "When you are with Goethe, I advise you to open your eyes and ears wide, and after you come home, if you can't repeat every word that fell from his mouth, I will have nothing more to do with you."

It is certain young Felix did repeat every word that fell from Goethe's mouth. Mendelssohn had a phenomenal memory. In 1829 his overture to *A Midsummer-Night's Dream* was performed in England. The score was carelessly left in a hackney coach and disappeared. It turned up *100 years* later at the Royal Academy. Mendelssohn seemed not a bit disturbed by the loss of his music. Immediately he sat down and rewrote the whole overture from memory and every note agreed with the orchestra parts.

It was through Zelter that Mendelssohn learned to appreciate Bach. When Mendelssohn was only 12 he had already studied Bach's *St. Matthew Passion* in manuscript form in the Royal Library, and he became so excited about his discovery that his mother had a copy made for him as a birthday present. Eight years later in 1829 Mendelssohn performed Bach's *St. Matthew Passion* in Berlin, and it is considered one of the great events in the history of music.

The *St. Matthew Passion* was given the second time on Bach's birthday, the 21st of March, and it again met with great success. Mendelssohn said to a friend in the theater who had helped him to persuade Zelter to perform the passion, "To think that it should be an actor and a Jew that had given back to the people the greatest Christian work."

Mendelssohn, in contrast to the modern school which underrates the music of the past, insisted one should learn from such masters as Bach and Handel without being merely imitative. Perhaps more than any other conductor, Mendelssohn contributed to shaping audiences' taste for good music. He had excellent musical taste himself and demanded excellence in performance. Besides renewing interest in Bach and Handel, Mendelssohn also deserves credit for increasing the performances of works by Mozart and Beethoven.

Felix Mendelssohn was born in Hamburg, Germany in 1809. The son of wealthy, cultured Jewish parents who had become Lutherans, Mendelssohn was baptized in the Lutheran Church. In 1812 the family moved to Berlin. Both he and his sister, Fanny, were taught music by their capable mother. In the Mendelssohn family the tradition of hard work was strongly established, and self-indulgence played no part in Mendelssohn's life. All through his life he felt an almost religious devotion to his family in general and to the father particularly as the head of the family.

The grandfather, Moses Mendelssohn, was a well-known philosopher. It is a great tribute to his personality that in the face of much racial prejudice at the time of Frederick the Great, he was so widely loved and respected. Mendelssohn's father said of himself after his son became a well-known composer, pianist, and conductor, "Formerly I was known as the son of my father, and now the father of my son!" Even though Abraham was less distinguished than his father and his son, he was a remarkable character too and a man full of deep family affection.

Of all the composers we have considered, Felix Mendelssohn seems to have been the most versatile. He could paint and draw excellently. He also was a bit of a literary artist as judged by his letters and occasional poems. He was an all-around athlete, and musically, he had many talents. He was a composer and conductor, and he played the piano and organ amazingly well and was more than an adequate performer on the violin and viola.

Clara Schumann, the famous German pianist, once said, "My recollections of Mendelssohn's playing are among the most delightful things in my artistic life. . . . He could carry one with him in the most incredible manner, and his playing was always stamped with beauty and nobility." Being able to do so many things, and to do them well, placed a burden on Mendelssohn. He tended to do too many things, and this plus his natural restless temperament and the emotional tensions which are a part of creativity, sometimes resulted in a rather ineffectual fussiness in some of this music.

If there is one thing great musicians have in common, it is their irritability. Being "sensitive" does not alone prove that an individual is a great artist, but as Einstein explains in his book *Greatness In Music,* "The irritability of the great is caused by the task to which they are committed, and the urge to accomplish that task to the utmost degree."

In 1829 Mendelssohn made the first of ten trips to England. He achieved almost immediate fame as a composer, conductor, and soloists. Even today, Mendelssohn's works are admired and performed more in England than in any other country. His conservatism, melodiousness, high spirits, and unfailing good manners appealed to the British and still do.

He introduced Beethoven's Concerto in E Flat to English audiences, and on another visit, the Concerto in G. Mendelssohn was one of the first artists to play a concerto by heart in public. That he was a modest man in spite of his giftedness and high standing in society is illustrated when at a concert the score for one of his trios was mislaid. Mendelssohn put another volume upside down on the music stand and had a friend turn the pages in order that he might not seem to be playing by heart when his colleagues had to have notes.

Fingal's Cave or *The Hebrides* Overture was composed when Mendelssohn was 21. It was written after a visit to the Hebrides, and it is one of his finest works. He loved to travel, and often was inspired by things which he saw and experienced during his journeys. He said once, "To me the finest thing in nature is the sea."

His wonderful conducting of the festival at Düsseldorf in 1832 led to his appointment as general music-director to the town. Here he began his first oratorio, *St. Paul.* Then he received an invitation to take the permanent direction of the Gewandhaus concerts at Leipzig. This was the highest musical position in Germany, and finally in 1835 Mendelssohn went to Leipzig where he was received with acclamation. Shortly after his arrival there he had a welcome visit from Chopin, and about the same time he met Robert Schumann and Schumann's future wife, Clara.

In 1837 Mendelssohn married Cecile Jeanrenaud, a minister's daughter from Frankfurt. They had five children. His wife was reserved in contrast to Mendelssohn's warm, outgoing personality, but she had great charm, serenity, and good sense. She was an oil painter, and the best of wives for Mendelssohn. They were a devoted couple.

In 1841 the King of Prussia called Mendelssohn to Berlin and gave him the title of *Kapellmeister.* It was an honor, and the composer, not wanting to seem ungrateful, found it difficult to turn down; but the appointment soon became a vexation and a strain. His early death was definitely related to overwork.

The high point of Mendelssohn's visit to England in 1842 was his invitation to perform for Queen Victoria at the palace. While waiting for her to appear, Mendelssohn and Prince Albert were having an animated conversation, hauling out all manner of volumes of music. Suddenly the young Queen arrived and seeing books and portfolios scattered about the room, immediately began to tidy up the royal chamber. After Mendelssohn played for the Queen, Prince Albert urged her to sing. It took awhile to find the music, and Queen Victoria performed to Mendelssohn's accompaniment. She sang in a small but well-trained voice, making a few mistakes and admitting that her nervousness made her short of breath. The visit gave great pleasure to all three. In a letter to his family Mendelssohn described Queen Victoria as "pretty, shyly friendly and polite, and speaks German very well. Her singing is quite delightful."

Mendelssohn in 1843 founded the great conservatory in Leipzig, and two years later he introduced Jenny Lind to the Gewandhaus concerts. He wrote the soprano solo "Hear Ye Israel" for the famous Swedish singer whom Mendelssohn admired greatly. At the height of her career Jenny Lind left the opera stage to devote her life to oratorio singing. As Radcliffe relates the incident, a friend asked her, "How was it that you ever came to abandon the stage at the very height of your success?" She replied, "When every day it made me think less of the Bible what else could I do?"

The outstanding instrument of the Romantic era was the piano just as the organ was for the Baroque and the tape recorder (electronic music) is for the 20th century. Mendelssohn's *Songs Without Words,* a series of small, intimate piano pieces, contributed enormously to his popularity. His elegant and sensitive style is essentially classical.

His well-known symphonies, the *Scottish* and the *Italian,* show the high quality of Mendelssohn's orchestration and mastery of form. In the *Reformation* Symphony, written for the tercentenary of the Augsburg Protestant Confession, Mendelssohn used Luther's "A Mighty Fortress is Our God" during the last movement. Of his 200 musical compositions, one of the favorites today is his Concerto for Violin in E Minor. It is considered one of the finest of all violin concertos.

Mendelssohn was the greatest 19th century composer of oratorios, and like Bach and Handel he knew the Bible well. He said often, "The Bible is always the best of all." His oratorio *St. Paul* is based on a pure and simple Scriptural text. His use of the chorale suggests the influence of Bach.

Mendelssohn always loved England and made many successful trips there. His oratorio *Elijah* (the greatest oratorio since Handel's *Messiah*) was composed for the English public. He was an excellent writer for the chorus. Like Handel, Mendelssohn could write moving and effective choral music—for instance, the "Baal" choruses or the lovely "He Watching over Israel." "If With All Your Heart You Truly Seek Him," "Lift Thine Eyes," and "He That Shall Endure to the End" are Mendelssohn at his best. The oratorio *Elijah* is a work of the greatest stylistic purity and the highest nobility. It dramatically demonstrates his Christian faith.

Elijah was a great success in England. It was first given in 1846 as a morning performance in the Birmingham festival. The moment the beloved Mendelssohn took his place as conductor of the oratorio, the sun broke forth. The audience spontaneously burst into applause at the dramatic effect, and they continued to applaud throughout the performance; even so, the meticulous Mendelssohn made many revisions before publication. He remained a highly fastidious composer to the end, and one of the most intelligent and scholarly composers of the century. Within less than two years after the Birmingham triumph, Mendelssohn was dead at the age of 38. He had been devoted to his gifted sister, Fanny, and what hastened his death was receiving the abrupt news of her death only six months before his. He fell into a state of unconsciousness and never fully recovered.

The music of Felix Mendelssohn breathes goodness and happiness. His name Felix means "the happy one." He was a gifted person, and he used his gifts to the glory of God. All Europe sorrowed over the loss of this amazing man and musician. It was almost like an international calamity, because Mendelssohn with his personal charm and shining Christian purity had left his mark. Some of Mendelssohn's music has faded, and some lacks depth, but the best is on a high level and fills us with admiration. "He That Shall Endure to the End" is not only an inspiration to listen to, but it is great music.

Recommended Reading
Radcliffe, Philip. *Mendelssohn.* London: J. M. Dent, 1957.

Recommended Listening
Concerto in E Minor for Violin
Elijah
A Midsummer-Night's Dream
A Midsummer-Night's Dream, Incidental Music
Octet in E flat for Strings
Hebrides Overture
Rondo Brillante for Piano and Orchestra, Op. 29
Songs Without Words
Symphony No. 3, *Scotch*
Symphony No. 4, *Italian*
Symphony No. 5, *Reformation*
Variations Serieuses
Sonatas for Organ

Chapter X

Richard Wagner

(1813—1883)

"He rejected history and chose mythology creating a world of his own."—Lang

Richard Wagner was familiar with the theater from childhood. His step-father, Ludwig Geyer, probably of Jewish blood, whom historians as well as Wagner regarded as his real father, was a gifted actor, singer, and artist. As early as 10, Wagner was studying Greek tragedy (so he said). When he learned English he promptly fell in love with Shakespeare. One of Wagner's first literary ventures was "Leubald and Adelaide," a bloody tragedy vaguely reminiscent of *Hamlet*. The young Wagner had so many dead characters in the first act he had to bring them back as ghosts to complete the drama.

His musical interests had a slow awakening. His talent for music as a youth was so unpromising that his piano teacher said, "Nothing will ever come of *him*." But in 1827 his lifelong passion for Beethoven's music was aroused by his attending the Gewandhaus concerts in Leipzig. He was particularly stirred by hearing Beethoven's Ninth Symphony. Later Wagner said that his operas were a continuation of Beethoven's Ninth Symphony.

He studied music secretly, learning counterpoint from Beethoven, orchestration from Mozart, and harmony by instinct. Wagner was regarded as an "intelligent but lazy" pupil. At 18 he entered Leipzig University and studied briefly with Weinlig, a successor of Bach at the St. Thomas Church, but he continued to be an erratic and careless student and interrupted his studies with frequent drinking bouts, gambling, and affairs with women. The theater was his world, and loose living was part of it.

He was offered a post as musical director at Magdeburg, and there he fell in love with the actress, Minna Planer. Although she was uncultured, she was experienced in the life of the theater. They finally married after two years of living together, but their marriage was a torture for both of them. Wagner's years of Bohemianism had encouraged a pattern of irresponsibility, extravagance, and dishonesty which was to become a way of life for him.

Six months after their marriage, Minna left him; but she rejoined him in Riga when Wagner was appointed the music director of the theater in 1837. Wagner wrote most of *Rienzi* there. But after two years with debts piled high, the Wagners fled Russia, by way of the Norwegian fiords and across the channel to England. The composer, inspired by the storms they encountered while aboard ship, conceived the idea for his next opera, *The Flying Dutchman,* which is outstanding for its musical description of a storm-tossed sea, and the theme of salvation through the love of a woman.

The next three years in Paris were a time of poverty and misery, but he wrote *The Flying Dutchman* during this period. No obstacle could hinder his creativity. The word "impossible" was unknown to Wagner. He arrived in Paris full of hope, but everything soured. He quickly ran out of money, and he and Minna lived in quarters far worse than anything they had experienced in their fifth-rate theatrical world in Germany. "The almost incredible bitterness of the Paris years left an indelible mark," writes Abraham, "as large as it was ugly, on Wagner's soul."* After experiencing poverty in Paris, Wagner seemed bent on never knowing want again. His love of luxury and living above his means on other people's money kept him constantly in debt, but it was no great burden to him. He simply borrowed more money from friends, relatives, and strangers he had charmed, without a thought of paying them back. Wagner believed the world owed him a living—and a good one at that.

In 1843 after *Rienzi* and *The Flying Dutchman* were performed successfully, Wagner was offered the coveted position of conductor of the Royal Theater in Dresden. There he remained six years. With his restless nature he was never content, but he did write *Tannhäuser* (1845) and *Lohengrin* (1848), two masterly treatments of the Romantic view of medieval life. The conflict between the two worlds, the world of the flesh and that of the spirit, was Wagner's basic subject so clearly dealt with in these operas. Besides composing the music, Wagner wrote all the words for his operas. *Lohengrin* was the last important German Romantic opera, and we see changes prophetic of the music dramas of Wagner's next period. *Lohengrin* was first performed in Weimar under the direction of Franz Liszt in 1850. Liszt was a champion of Wagner's music and later became his father-in-law.

Richard Wagner was the key figure of Romanticism in which we have the abandonment of categories. He was in search of the unattainable Romantic ideal, the universal, all-embracing art-work. Wagner was a born reformer, an

---

*Gerald Abraham, *A Hundred Years of Music* (New York), 1938

insatiable idealist, and a monumental egoist set out to create a world of his own, but his egomania was supported by genius. Romanticism by nature must be fragmentary with its longing for the infinite which cannot be attained. Wagner was one of the first philosophical composers placing mythology in the central position of his romantic thought. Like Nietzsche, Wagner felt that mankind was in need of a new mythology. He felt that history was insufficient for the purpose of art. Even in his youth Wagner had the dramatist's instinct to seek escape from this world by contriving another, and we shall see later that in *The Ring* he created his own world of mythology.

In 1849 social revolution was brewing in Germany, and Wagner participated in an unsuccessful revolution. A warrant was issued for his arrest, and he fled to Switzerland and was in exile there for the next 10 years.

During his first years in Switzerland, Wagner wrote no music. Always an omnivorous reader, Wagner began to examine his own thinking on subjects ranging from anti-Semitism to vegetarianism. These *Swiss Essays* reveal how unbalanced, yet brilliant, egocentric, and calloused Wagner really was. In his essay "Jewishness in Music" Wagner advocated the complete elimination of the Jews from German society and culture, though later Jewish musicians were some of his finest interpreters. As Sigmund Spaeth once commented, "It is easy to like the music of Richard Wagner; it is almost impossible to like him as a man." Finally Wagner came back to his music, and in 1853 he began the libretto for his monumental creation, *The Ring of the Nibelung.*

In 1857, still unable to go back to Germany, Wagner and his wife Minna were invited to live in a cottage near Zurich on the estate of Otto Wesendonck, a wealthy industrialist. Wagner, who was not only in his music but in his life "looking for salvation in the ideal woman," thought he found her in the person of the beautiful wife of his benefactor. Matilde Wesendonck returned the love of the composer who seems to have had an hypnotic fascination for practically all women, and even a number of men. This ugly little man with his protruding forehead, prominent nose and mouth, must have caused a stir every time he came into a room. Having been in the theater all his life he demanded to be the center of attention, and in spite of his immoral character, he had remarkable personal magnetism. His own life would make a fascinating opera story.

In this latest "love" interval Matilde Wesendonck wrote five poems which Wagner set to music. Some of this music was later included in *Tristan,* which Wagner was then working on. He wrote the libretto in four weeks, an astonishing feat. The affair was eventually discovered by Wagner's enraged wife who intercepted a love letter. Wagner was forced to flee to Venice where he wrote the yearning second act of *Tristan* inspired by his violent desire for Matilde. In this opera the passion of love becomes almost a delirium with its ever-intensifying chromaticisms, its unbroken deluge of emotion. Completed in 1859, *Tristan* is a unique conception for the stage. It deals with the emotional lives of the characters rather than the external events or actions. There is not one happy note in it. Schnorr, the first to sing the role of Tristan, died after four performances at the age of 29.

There is tragic gloom in the music, and yet as Grout says, "*Tristan* is in many respects the quintessence of Wagner's mature style. Few works in the history of music have exerted so potent an influence on succeeding generations of composers." And yet when *Tristan* was first performed, all that many critics could see and hear were two large people screaming at each other!

According to Thomas Mann a great event in Wagner's life was his becoming acquainted with the philosophy of Schopenhauer, particularly his masterpiece, *The World as Will and Idea.* It was the uniting of two brilliant but neurotic minds. Schopenhauer was a cynical, solitary man influenced by Eastern religions, but basically his philosophy is atheistic. For him blind will is the ultimate reality. Schopenhauer sought relief from suffering through the contemplation of works of art, especially music. He preached the worship of heroes. He saw the ultimate good in beauty and ultimate joy in creating or cherishing the beautiful.

Wagner's discovery of Schopenhauer confirmed his own instinctive pessimism. His preoccupation with *The World as Will and Idea* and his yearning for Matilde Wesendonck brought forth *Tristan.* The second act of the opera is filled with Schopenhauer's pessimistic philosophy of hopeless love longing for night, death, and oblivion. Lang says, "The music of romanticism reached its peak and its ruin in Wagner." Richard Wagner was one of the most influential personalities of the 19th century, and what came out of his mind has altered the course of history. He wrote for the illness of the 19th century and furnished a magic potion: his seductiveness.

One of many talented artists influenced by Wagner was the French poet Baudelaire. He had two gods—Poe and Wagner. Baudelaire spoke of Wagner's music and its "opium influence" on him. He tried to imitate Wagner by living a life free from restraints and longing for the unattainable. Baudelaire, his mind destroyed by drugs and alcohol, died paralyzed at the age of 46 because of a venereal disease; he wrote from his deathbed, ". . . feeling the wind of the wings of madness."

In 1860 Wagner went to Paris where the productions of *Tannhäuser* were fiascos owing to riots by members of an influential group, the Jockey Club, angered because the opera lacked the traditional second-act ballet. Wagner then spent three years in Vienna traveling widely as a conductor, but again was forced to flee the city to avoid imprisonment for debts. Trying to explain his conduct, his irresponsible way of living, Wagner said, "mine is a highly susceptible, intense, voracious sensuality, which must somehow or another be indulged if my mind is to accomplish the agonizing labor of calling a non-existent world into being."

At the most desperate moment in his life, Wagner was summoned to meet the 19-year-old King Ludwig II who had just come to the throne of Bavaria. The date was May 3, 1864. Ludwig, a very unstable man himself, had already come under the "opium" spell of Wagner's music. The young king promised Wagner financial independence and that his every artistic wish would be satisfied. If Ludwig had not entered the scene at this time, the later works of Wagner probably would not have been written. He moved to Munich and enjoyed a short period of triumph where many of his operas were performed. But Wagner's insistence on luxurious surroundings, rooms filled with priceless rugs, paintings, velvet and satin hangings, and his profligate life had a negative influence on King Ludwig politically and incensed the Bavarian people. Wagner was forced to leave, but his music continued to be the obsession of Ludwig's life. Later the king helped build the Wagnerian Theater in Bayreuth before he lost his mind, was deposed, and committed suicide by drowning at the age of 41. The extraordinary castles that Ludwig designed, such as Neuschwanstein with its Wagnerian rooms are worth visiting.

In his 53rd year Wagner returned to Switzerland, and with money from King Ludwig he secured a home at Triebschen on Lake Lucerne. Wagner had already had a child by Cosima von Bülow, the wife of the first great Wagnerian conductor, and she and the child came with him to Triebschen. The disillusioned husband said, "If it had been anyone but Wagner, I would have shot him." Cosima, the illegitimate daughter of Liszt, became Wagner's mistress, and they had three children. Finally they were married in 1870 after von Bülow granted a divorce. (Minna had died of a heart attack in 1866.)

Wagner believed that a woman fulfills her highest qualities in sacrificing herself for man, and Cosima did this in a complete sense. She was the ideal, self-effacing, and worshipful wife essential to Wagner's creativity. In the beautiful home at Triebschen Wagner spent some of his happiest and most creative years, if a person like Wagner could ever be said to be happy. Here he completed the opera *Die Meistersinger,* and started his two-volume autobiography, which wallows in self-deception and is a very twisted view of the facts.

One of many distinguished visitors at Lake Lucerne was the philosopher, Nietzsche. As a boy of 14 he fell in love with the music of Wagner. Nietzsche is known as the apostle of the Superman and the prophet of doom. He predicted the end of the common man, and being a child of Darwin, Nietzsche created a god in his own image. Nietzsche along with Schopenhauer believed that human behavior is irrational and the answer lay in Superman, that is, the developing of an aristocratic, ruthless, superior human race which could dominate the world. In Wagner's music dramas Nietzsche saw a revivifying of the pagan power which he thought would triumph over the disintegrating weakness of the "meek" Christian tradition.

After Wagner wrote *Parsifal* Nietzsche attacked his former friend in a paper entitled, "The Case of Wagner," accusing the composer of making music ill. Nietzsche misinterpreted *Parsifal.* He thought it had Christian overtones, but quite the contrary. Wagner was not bowing down to Christ. Some parts of the work are considered among the finest music composed on a religious theme, especially the "Prelude" and the "Good Friday Spell," but even though the plot involves the sword with which Christ was struck during the crucifixion and the chalice used at the Last Supper, this in no way makes it a Christian opera.

What it is, is typically Romantic music infused with idealistic longings that might be called "religious" in a vague pantheistic sense. The American Wagner critic, Robert W. Gutman, points out that Wagner clearly detested Christianity which he saw as "Judaic error perpetuated."

Finally we have arrived at Wagner's immense work *The Ring of the Nibelungen* which is the most monumental musical achievement to weather the test of time. It took Wagner 26 years to complete. The libretto of *The Ring,* which includes *Das Rheingold, Die Walküre, Siegfried,* and *Die Götterdämmerung,* was conceived backwards. The basic theme of the cycle concerns the desire for world power and gold, and it ends in destruction.

The musical fabric of *The Ring* is constructed of leading motifs, a type of musical label, with the ascending themes referring to life and the descending themes to death. These are woven into Wagner's technical method of continuous music and filled with psychological meaning. The stupendous climax of *The Ring* is Brünnhilde's immolation scene.

Wagner's desire was to merge the different arts, poetry, dance, music, and painting into one super-experience. He sought to express a world philosophy in music drama—the "universal art work" capable of freeing modern man. He believed that human redemption was achieved by love, but because of his humanistic base it ends in pessimism with everyone being destroyed. Wagner's concept of man finding redemption through a woman leads to death. God's love for the world through Christ and whosoever believes in Him, leads to life everlasting.

The will to power that the philosopher, Nietzsche, preached helped Hitler bring on the holocaust of World War II, and it should not surprise us that Hitler's favorite composer was Wagner. He refused to listen to anything except the Nordic music dramas of Richard Wagner and military bands. I read recently that Hitler hailed Wagner as his only predecessor.

Wagner's 13 operas generally have superb beginnings and endings with much too much in between. There are stretches of boredom, loudness, and bigness. His music dramas are static, heavy, and at times tedious, but they have a sweep, grandeur, and spaciousness uniquely their own. Undoubtedly, Wagner has written some of the most exalted music ever composed which enchants and over-powers the senses. The orchestra is of central importance. He enlarged the resources of the orchestra enormously and created a vast new musical language. Suffering and sorrow constitute the basic tone of the music dramas. There is little humor in Wagner's life or music with the exception of *Die Meistersinger.*

Richard Wagner, the man of iron determination, con-troversy, and raw energy became more inconsiderate (if that is possible), self-obsessed, and melancholy as he grew older. By this time he was living at Wahnfried in Bayreuth with frequent trips to Italy to find relief for his skin dis-ease, erysipelas. Finally he was able to construct his "tem-ple" at Bayreuth, and the first festival was held in 1876 with resounding success. Wagner died in 1883 in Venice at the Vendramin Palace of a heart attack and he was buried at Wahnfried. His was an obsession to an artistic ideal that over-rode all other obligations, but his music lives on in the great theaters of the world. Crowds flock to Bayreuth every summer to hear his colossal music dramas.

In Louis Untermeyer's excellent book, *Makers of the Modern World,* the first four men he writes about are Dar-win, Kierkegaard, Wagner, and Karl Marx. Untermeyer opens his essay on Wagner with these words: "A self-pampered voluptuary who preached the gospel of self-denial and renunciation, an unscrupulous opportunist who, deceiving his wife, assured her that 'your suffering will be rewarded by my fame,' an importunate cadger who was also an accomplished cad, Richard Wagner not only changed the whole course of modern music but built a monumental edifice which has withstood the controversial assaults of battering animosity, critical scorn and wildly changing taste."* When you listen to the music of Wagner, be aware of his "opium" influence.

Recommended Reading

Newman, Ernest. *Wagner as Man and Artist.* New York: Garden City Publishing Co., 1941.

Osborne, Charles. *Wagner and his World.* London: Thames and Hudson, 1977.

Recommended Listening

Götterdämmerung (The Ring)
  "Funeral Music"
  "Rhine Journey"
  "Immolation Scene"
Lohengrin—Preludes
Die Meistersinger—Preludes
Parsifal—Good Friday Music
Siegfried Idyll
Tannhäuser—Overture
Tristan and Isolde—Prelude and Liebestod
Die Walküre (The Ring)
  "Magic Fire Music"
  "Ride of the Valkyries"
Wesendonck Songs
Wagner arias

*L. Untermeyer, *Makers of the Modern World* (New York: Simon and Schuster, 1966), p. 12.

Chapter XI

Giuseppe Verdi
(1813—1901)

"The man that hath no music in himself, Nor is moved with concord of sweet sounds, Is fit for treason, stratagems, and spoils."—Shakespeare

A few months after Giuseppe Verdi was born in Italy, Russian and Austrian soldiers swept down from the north killing as many people as they could seize. To protect herself and her child, Luisa Verdi found refuge in the village church in a narrow staircase to the belfry, and thereby saved herself and the future composer. It is said that Verdi's operas are performed more often today than those of any other composer.

Verdi was born in 1813 in Le Roncole, a tiny village in the province of Parma, at that time occupied by the French. His father kept a small inn that was also a sort of village store. They were poor people, peasants actually, but to be a peasant in Italy is not demeaning. A national characteristic of these humble people is the humane spirit found among them. Italians are kindhearted, hospitable folk who laugh and cry easily. They have a strong feeling of solidarity which makes poverty bearable. They are quick to help each other.

The parents of Verdi were not musical, but when their son showed an interest in learning, the father bought an old spinet, and the boy pounded on it with great delight. Verdi received the rudiments of his musical education from the village organist in the same church where his mother had saved his life. The organist was impressed with the boy's exceptional gifts, and when the organist died suddenly, Verdi at the age of 12, was able to succeed him.

As a boy, Verdi used to visit the neighboring town of Busseto where his father bought supplies from Antonio Barezzi, a well-to-do shopkeeper. Barezzi liked the boy and took him into his shop. As Barezzi was also a lover of music, through him Verdi was put in touch with other musicians who were able to teach him what they knew. In a few years Verdi became the assistant conductor in Busseto and was a person of some importance in town. As early as 16 Verdi was writing songs, piano pieces, church music, and particularly marches, which were played by the Busseto Municipal Band to great applause.

When Verdi was 18, he tried to get the position as organist in a larger town nearby, but he failed. However, by this time the general feeling in Busseto was that young Verdi was very talented musically and should go to Milan and study at the Conservatory. He was granted some money from a music fund in Busseto, and his friend and future father-in-law, Barezzi, added a contribution of his own.

In 1831 Verdi arrived in Milan excited about being able to study at the Music Conservatory, but he was refused admission on the grounds that he lacked sufficient musical knowledge and that he was too old to begin studying. The 18-year-old Verdi was bitterly disappointed, but he was a tough-minded young man who did not easily accept defeat, and soon he became the private pupil of the composer Vincenzo Lavigna, who gave him a solid grounding in the music of Palestrina and Marcello, taught him harmony and counterpoint, and everything he knew about opera. Best of all they became friends.

After three years of study in Milan, Verdi returned to Busseto, and in 1835 he married Margherita Barezzi. They had known and cared for each other since Verdi as a boy began to work for her father. At this time Verdi was composing an opera, and he hoped to have it produced in Parma. But it was rejected so in 1839 Verdi, his wife and two small children moved to Milan.

Again he met with disappointment. His opera was accepted, but soon after rehearsals began, the tenor fell ill, and the production had to be postponed. This discouraged Verdi so much he decided to return to Busseto, but his wife and Merelli, the new Impresario at La Scala, persuaded him to remain in Milan and to try again. It was not that Verdi lacked confidence, but he had a wife and two children to care for. Verdi had a strong sense of doing what was right, which included not being obligated to others to support him. Finally, in November of 1839 Verdi's *Oberto* was produced. As Verdi himself said about the opera, "It was not very great, but good enough."

It lead to a commission. He was asked to write a comic opera, *King for a Day.* Just as he began to write it, Verdi fell ill with angina, and his wife cared for him through difficult and anxious weeks. They were poor, and it was a burden to Verdi that he could not pay the rent on time, not being well enough to do anything about it. Margherita pawned her last trinkets and paid the rent, and after awhile Verdi was able to work again. But soon complete disaster struck the loving family. Between 1838 and 1840 Verdi's two children and wife died. These sudden tragedies were so shocking to him that years later when he was telling a friend what had happened to him when he first moved to

Milan, Verdi thought his wife and children had all died within three months rather than two years. Ever afterwards he was inclined to melancholy.

In this black time in his life, Verdi was reduced to the point of despair. He sent back to Busseto the furniture and small effects his wife had carefully and lovingly collected for their little home in Milan, and he moved into a dismal furnished room on the Piazzeta San Romano. He had one friend who occasionally visited him, and Verdi would mumble something about taking students, but he never did. Most of the time he was alone, eating alone at a dreary *trattoria* on the piazza or having a "sea biscuit" dipped in water in his room. To add to the grimness of these months, he had to finish the comic opera.

King for a Day was produced in 1840, and it was a complete fiasco. People booed and hissed which is a frightful but all too common experience in an Italian opera house. It left Verdi stunned and resentful, having recently endured such deep personal tragedy. He said years later that if the audience had only endured the opera in silence he could have borne that. This experience affected his outlook on life and art during the rest of his career, and his immediate reaction was never to compose again.

In his biography of Verdi, Toye recounts this crucial incident in the composer's life: Finally Merelli at La Scala knew something had to be done, and he sent for Verdi. As Verdi said years later, "He treated me like a capricious child! . . . He refused to believe I could turn my back on music because of a single failure." But Verdi, still in mourning for his wife and children, was also adamant and continued to give no thought to composing as he found no consolation in it.

Time dragged on. "One evening in the winter as I was leaving the Galleria," Verdi said, "I ran into Merelli who was on his way to the theatre. It was snowing with large flakes. Taking me by the arm, he asked me to accompany him to his office at La Scala. We chatted as we went, and he told me of his troubles with a new opera he had to produce."

Merelli went into great detail about the opera, and when Verdi was about to leave, Merelli put the troublesome, thick manuscript into Verdi's hands. When he got to his room, Verdi threw the manuscript on the table, and the libretto fell open to these words, *"Va, pensiero, sull'ali dorate"* (Go, thought, on golden wings). As Verdi said, "I glanced through the verses following and was deeply moved, particularly because they almost paraphrased the Bible which I have always loved to read." Verdi read the libretto three times, and *Nabucco* kept running in his head all night.

However, Verdi, still determined never to compose again, returned the manuscript to Merelli, but Merelli, even more determined, stuffed the libretto back in Verdi's overcoat pocket while shouting, "Put it to music, put it to music!" He shoved the composer out of the office and locked the door. Again Verdi went home with *Nabucco* in his pocket. He later explained how he composed the music, "Today a verse; tomorrow another; one time a note, another a phrase . . . little by little the opera was done."

In three months, Verdi had completed *Nabucco,* the opera destined to be the foundation of Verdi's fame and fortune. The story is about Nebuchadnezzar, but for purpose of song his name is changed to Nabucco. It was the best of Verdi's early operas and with excellent singers it was a great success. To understand why Verdi became famous so quickly one must understand the political climate in Italy at this time. The Italians were weary of being under the heel of the Austrians, and the wonderful chorus, "Go, Thought, on Golden Wings," which concerns the longing of the Jewish exiles for home and freedom became the perfect expression for the emotional Italians longing for their independence. *Nabucco* was premiered March 9,

1842 and from then on Verdi, who was himself a fiery patriot, became a national hero, idolized as no composer had ever been. Verdi became a symbol of Italy's struggle for independence from Austria in the mid-1800's. With strictly enforced censorship the Italian people had no way to express their great desire to be free, and so "Viva Verdi" became a popular war cry throughout Italy, for the Italians associated the letters in Verdi's last name with the slogan, "Vittorio Emmanuele Re d'Italia" (Victor Emmanuel King of Italy), and in 1861 Victor Emmanuel was crowned King of Italy.

One of the outstanding singers in the *Nabucco* opera was Guiseppina Strepponi who, after a scandal-ridden interlude, became Verdi's devoted second wife. She brought love, stability, and a reason to go on back into the life of Verdi. Also what helped to draw out the alternately shy, fierce, and stubborn composer, were the "salons" held in the home of the Contessa Maffei. She was an intelligent woman with gentle manners, and she saw the worth of the young composer who had experienced such sorrow. She became a good and kind friend. It speaks well of Verdi's self-education that he could hold his own among the intellectuals who attended the salons. But by nature Verdi was taciturn, and he became a favorite as good listeners are always popular among those who love to talk! These evenings stimulated, taught, and disciplined Verdi.

The operas of Verdi's early period are clearly influenced by Rossini, Bellini, and Donizetti, but they also reveal his own extraordinary lyrical and dramatic gifts which so ably generate genuine theatrical excitement. There were several productive years after *Nabucco*. In 1847 Verdi took a definite step forward and chose a theme from Shakespeare. The result was the opera *Macbeth*. Verdi had a lifelong attraction to Shakespeare, but he had to wait 40 years before he found the right librettist.

By 1853 Verdi had composed his three most popular

and widely performed operas, *Rigoletto, Il Trovatore,* and *La Traviata.* These were epoch-making works. When *La Traviata* was first performed in Venice, it was a complete failure. It was not the fault of the opera. It was because of poor casting. The soprano, who is the main character, was *very* stout, and the audience broke out into roars of laughter in the tragic scene when the doctor announces that she is in the last stages of consumption and has only a few hours to live.

Verdi, in his composing, never broke with the past or experimented radically with new ideas. He said at one time, "Let us return to the old; it will be an advance." This became a famous maxim. He also said that he was not a learned composer, only a very experienced one.

Verdi was a sound businessman, honest, true to his word, and thoroughly competent to deal with impresarios, publishers, and prima donnas and tenors. As soon as he was financially able he bought a farm near Busseto. This was no whim of the composer. He said of himself after he became famous, "I am and always will be a Le Roncole peasant."

All his life Verdi loved the land in that corner of Parma where he was born. He is the only eminent composer in history who was also a successful farmer. Around his own country home, Sant' Agata, Verdi developed a model farm which gave employment to 200 farmers and their families. When times were hard, instead of lowering salaries, he raised their wages. Verdi, like Handel, did not forget those who helped him when he was poor. He provided well for his relatives and frequently sent gifts to those who had a need.

Because of his love for the country and seclusion, Verdi retained his simplicity. He loved Sant'Agata best of all with his superb horses and dogs, but because it was cold and damp in the winter, Verdi rented an apartment in Genoa for his wife's sake. But they never could stay very long at either place as there were always rehearsals and performances in Milan, Rome, Venice, Paris, and other European cities.

Nearly every year Verdi brought out another opera, and one year, even three. They were not all successful, but the faults nearly always stemmed from poor librettos. Verdi said, "In the theater the public will stand for anything but boredom." Therefore, even though some of the librettos are inferior and downright foolish, Verdi's operas continue to live, because they do have drama, no matter how primitive, and most of all, because they do have great music. In all Verdi wrote 26 operas.

To mention a few of the better known operas in the period between 1857-1871: *Simon Boccanegra,* first produced in Venice; *The Masked Ball,* Rome; *The Force of Destiny,* St. Petersburg; *Don Carlos,* Paris; and *Aïda,* composed for Cairo to celebrate the opening of the Suez Canal. As Aïda is dying, she sings, *"O terra addio, addio valle di pianti"* (literally, life is a vale of tears). The summing up of all Verdi was reaching for in his middle period is found in *Aïda,* called by some critics, the perfect grand opera.

For a long time Verdi was falsely considered a musical adversary of Richard Wagner (Both were born in 1813, and both composers died in Italy). Today one sees that Verdi is a totally different spirit with totally different aims, yet no less belonging to the "small company of great masters." Verdi admired Wagner's music, but because of his innate musicianship and Latin grace, he was intellectually and musically Wagner's antithesis. The orchestra of Verdi is always in the background, and there is the irresistible triumph of melody and voice. Because of his temperament and teaching Verdi despised excessive length.

There are scenes in all of Verdi's operas that may be counted among the most extraordinary and moving ever written. He was an explosive composer from the beginning to the end. What is decisive is Verdi's grandeur as an artist, his sincerity, and his integrity as a man. Verdi was always a conscientious craftsman. He felt that simplicity spells strength, and one hears it in his impassioned melodies. In his works Verdi shows that he is a totally committed artist. As Lang says, "Verdi's music is eternally human, bold, dramatic, full-bodied, and Italian in every atom." It will be seen that Verdi produced more slowly as the years went by, not because he lacked inspiration, but the works required a longer time for gestation. There was no longer the "guitar" accompaniment in the orchestra but richer, broader, more ambitious instrumentation.

In 1874 Verdi produced the Requiem Mass. It was to honor Italy's greatest prose writer, Alessandro Manzoni. His *I promessi sposi (The Betrothed)* was the most famous Italian novel of the 19th century. As Verdi said, "It is a truthful book, as true as truth itself." Verdi admired Manzoni from boyhood, and even after he became a famous composer, he always felt that Manzoni was above him. The Requiem is a colossal work, deeply moving, vividly dramatic, and glorious in sound. It is unlike any other requiem, and has been criticized by some for its theatricality. Verdi conducted it for the first time in Venice, and because of his sincerity it was an immediate and permanent success. To understand in depth the conversation of many Italians, it is helpful to read *The Betrothed* and listen to Verdi's operas, as Italians are forever spicing their talk with quotes from Manzoni or snatches of song from *La Traviata* or *Falstaff*.

In the 1870's Verdi seemed to have reached the summit of his career, and apart from supervising productions in Italy, he spent more and more time at Sant'Agata which he managed himself down to the smallest detail. For a few years he even sat in the Parliament as a member from Busetto. In his country home he had a library of several thousand volumes most of which he had evidently read.

He loved to read in the evenings. By his bedside were the complete works of Shakespeare, Dante, Byron, and Schiller. Also within reaching distance were his King James Bible, Milton's *Paradise Lost,* all kinds of dictionaries and histories, and the complete string quartets of Haydn, Mozart, and Beethoven.

In 1887, after a silence of 16 years, news spread around Milan that Verdi was writing another opera, this one to be set to a play by Shakespeare. Meeting the poet Arrigo Boito had fired the imagination of the 74-year-old composer. Today Boito ranks among the best librettists in the entire history of opera. He submitted the best libretto Verdi ever had for *Otello,* and in this work Verdi brought to fusion everything that he had learned in a lifetime. *Otello* is the greatest tragic opera to come out of Italy. In it Verdi proclaims the glory of the human voice. He was convinced that the voice has an inexhaustible capacity for expression.

But *Otello* was not Verdi's last triumph. Six years later he wrote another masterpiece, this time a comic opera, again using words from one of Shakespeare's plays. Verdi was close to 80, and as excited about doing *Falstaff* as anything he had written in his life. As Lang shows, it did not come from the top of his head: "What shall I say?" said Verdi in trying to explain it to a friend. "For forty years I have wanted to write a comic opera, and fifty years I have known *The Merry Wives of Windsor,* but the usual 'buts' stood in the way. At last Boito has settled all the 'buts' and has given me a libretto like no other."

As Ernest Newman says, "It was a piece of singular good fortune both for Verdi and for the world that at the height of the musician's imaginative and technical powers he should meet with a poet who could place Shakespeare at his service in a form thoroughly practical for the operatic stage." The first performance of *Falstaff* drew celebrities from all over the world, and from the beginning it has been recognized as one of the three or four masterpieces in comic opera.

Strepponi, Verdi's wife, lived to see the triumph of *Otello* and *Falstaff,* and then she died in 1897. He missed her deeply, but he did not suffer from loneliness. The years had taught Verdi to cherish solitude, and he believed passionately in privacy for himself and others. He spent his last years at Sant'Agata, Genoa, and Milan continuing the routine of his life. In Genoa, everyone knew the great Verdi, but the people also understood and respected his desire to be alone. When he would enter his usual café, everyone in the room would rise in his honor, bow, and then leave him alone.

In spite of his fame and fortune, there remained in Verdi something of the durability and resiliance of the peasant in his outlook upon life to the end. His last compositions were settings of sacred texts called *Quattro pezzi sacri* (Four Sacred Pieces). Verdi died of a stroke in Milan in 1901. He left the royalties from his works to the Casa Verdi, a home for aged musicians in Milan. It is called "The House of Rest," and it still continues today. He and his beloved wife are buried there. Verdi's was a long and glorious career. He lived a rich and honest life, filled with a deeply felt humanity. Above all he loved the human voice and farming.

Recommended Reading
Hussey, Dyneley. *Verdi.* London: J. M. Dent, 1948.

Toye, Francis. *Giuseppe Verdi: His Life and Works.* New York: Alfred A. Knopf, 1931.

Recommended Listening
Aïda (Nile Scene)
Un Ballo in Maschera ("Eri Tu")
Don Carlos ("O Don Fatale")
Falstaff ("All the World's a Jest")
La Forza del Destino ("Pace, Pace, Mio Dio")

Macbeth (Sleepwalking Scene)
Nabucco ("Va Pensiero Sull'ali Dorante")
Otello (Act I—Love Duet)
Requiem Mass
Rigoletto (Quartet, Caro Nome)
Simon Boccanegra ("Il Lacarato Spirito")
La Traviata ("Ah! Fors e Lui")
Il Trovatore ("Miserere")

Chapter XII
Johannes Brahms
(1833—1897)

"For all flesh is as grass, and all the glory of man as the flower of grass. The grass withereth, and the flower thereof falleth away: But the word of the Lord endureth for ever." I Peter 1:24, 25

At the age of 13 Johannes Brahms helped support his family by playing the piano in the lowest sorts of sailors' dance-halls, taverns, and restaurants in Hamburg. But since he detested wasting time, often he propped a book on the music rack in front of him. It did not take long for this unhealthy and questionable atmosphere to undermine his delicate constitution, and finally his father rescued him by securing for him a teaching position in a pleasant country village away from the narrow, dirty streets, dilapidated, over-crowded, age-blackened houses and taverns of the poor neighborhood in Hamburg where Brahms grew up. The change of air and environment helped him greatly, and years later he looked back on those cheerful months in Winsen among the happiest in his childhood. They helped to establish the rugged health he enjoyed most of his life.

Johannes Brahms was born in Hamburg in 1833. His father played the double bass in the civic orchestra, and he was the first to teach young Brahms the basic elements of music. But Brahms revealed such talent he had to be passed on to another teacher. He had two teachers as a boy. Friedrich Cossel and Eduard Marxen both recognized Brahms as remarkably gifted. They taught him well and without pay. Brahms made his debut as a pianist at 10.

The mother of Johannes was 17 years older than her husband. Though she was not well educated, she was a woman of great sensitivity and spiritual resources. Brahms was devoted to her. In spite of their poor circumstances, his parents did their best to create a secure home and to foster with understanding the natural talents of their children.

Even though he had many struggles in his early years, Brahms developed into an outstanding pianist. Nevertheless, he considered playing the piano an avocation since he was determined to devote himself mainly to composition as soon as he could afford it.

In 1853 Brahms accepted an engagement as accompanist to the Hungarian violinist, Reményi, for a concert tour. In Göttingen the piano on which Brahms was to play the Kreutzer Sonata by Beethoven was a half tone below the right pitch. Brahms transposed it from A to B Flat and played the part by memory doing it so skillfully that the great violinist, Joseph Joachim, who was in the audience was astonished and wanted to meet Brahms. Joachim immediately liked the shy and unpretentious 20-year-old Brahms, and a lifelong friendship began.

Joachim, happy to recommend such a talent, gave Brahms introductions to some of the leading musicians of the day, including Robert and Clara Schumann. After Brahms played some of his compositions for them, Robert Schumann wrote an enthusiastic report about Brahms in the *New Magazine for Music*. He proclaimed Brahms to be the great composer of the future "called forth to give the ideal expression of the time."

Schumann was also the first to recognize the genius of Chopin. Frédéric Chopin (1810-1849), born in Poland, was one of the most original, creative geniuses in musical history. He composed relatively little, but was born into a world suited to his prodigious talents. The Romantic period was the time of the gigantic piano virtuosos. Like a jeweler polishing rare gems, Chopin worked on his pieces until they were as perfect as he could make them. His études are landmarks in the history of piano music and are among his greatest works. Chopin made the piano sing. He was a great melodist, and he created a new realm of piano sound. There is no greater specialist than Chopin. One can nearly always recognize a Chopin composition. There is scarcely one in his repertoire that we could dispense with.

Because Robert Schumann was highly respected in the musical world, his endorsement of Brahms and Brahms' unusual individuality caused his name to become known, and the publication of his works was eagerly awaited. This is one of the rare instances in the history of music of an established composer recognizing the genius of a new-comer. Schumann was 23 years older than Brahms. From the first, Schumann tried to interest Brahms in composing a symphony. "The beginning is the main thing," he said. "If only one makes a beginning, then the end comes of itself." Brahms owed much of his early style in writing music to Schumann.

One cannot speak about Robert Schumann without mentioning his wife, Clara. She was the most celebrated woman pianist of her time. She was trained by her father, married Robert in 1840, and continued to tour after her marriage, furthering her husband's career by giving the first performance of many of his works.

Robert Schumann, because of several personal tragedies

in his life, showed signs of depression and even mental illness as early as 1843. He kept hearing the note "A" sounding in his ears. He recovered somewhat, and had several busy years, writing music, traveling and directing; but in 1854 he had a renewal of the symptoms that threatened him before. Besides hearing the ringing "A" he now imagined he heard voices too. He threw himself in the Rhine, but was rescued and spent his last years in a private asylum where he died in 1856.

When Brahms heard of the tragic circumstances, he moved to Düsseldorf to help Clara and her children, and he was a strength to them during this time. He stayed for several years, living on piano lessons, composing incessantly, but publishing little. A lifelong friendship developed between Clara Schumann and Brahms. After leaving Düsseldorf, Brahms continued to submit his compositions to her before publishing them.

Undoubtedly Johannes Brahms was very much in love with Clara Schumann. She was one of the most fascinating women of the 19th century, but they never married. She was 14 years older than Brahms, for one thing, and they both needed their freedom: She to give concerts to support her family, and he to compose. After 1856, Clara Schumann frequently played in England and became noted as an interpreter of Brahms' music.

Between the years 1853 and 1857, Brahms taught, toured as a pianist, and composed. From 1857 to 1860 he was a teacher and conductor at the small German court of Lippe-Detmold. Twice the position of conductor of the Philharmonic Orchestra in Hamburg became vacant, but Brahms was not appointed, and so he resolved to forget his hometown. In 1863 he went to Vienna.

Some years later he finally settled in the enchanting city of Vienna where he was stimulated by an artistic and congenial atmosphere. Vienna, called the "Queen of the Danube," is a world center for literature, music, and learning. The inner city's most renowned street is the Ringstrasse with its parks and lilac trees, its opera house, Imperial Palace, and the famous St. Stephen's Cathedral nearby. The Viennese people are known for their liveliness, charm, wit, and ability to enjoy life. Music is a necessity to them.

As soon as Brahms was financially able, he devoted more and more time to composing. His publisher and friend, Simrock, helped him achieve independence. He did not need a large income for himself as he felt more comfortable when leading a simple life. But Brahms did derive pleasure in helping others, notably, Anton Dvorak, and he was especially generous to his family. Brahms, who enjoyed a wide range of great literature, delighted in giving books to friends and relatives. There were also several struggling young musicians who secretly received financial gifts from Brahms, as did Clara Schumann and her children. He delighted in doing good secretly.

Johannes Brahms was a gruff, humorous, sometimes lonely individual touched with melancholy. His outlook on life, as of so many Romantics, was mingled with pessimism. He was a modest man, sane, and with a lovable personality. His stubby, plump appearance was often somewhat untidy, and he had long hair and untrimmed beard and mustache. His rough humor was bearish, and he had a temper if interrupted in his work. Privacy for Brahms was a ruling passion. He loved independence, solitude, and freedom. He set great store by undisturbed solitude, and his friends knew he was not to be bothered when he was working.

Basically he was kindhearted and had a sense of politeness which knew no class distinctions. There was no haughtiness in Brahms. As an example, while staying in an Italian inn on one of his working holidays, he would go about in stockinged feet in the evenings rather than keep a poor servant waiting to polish his boots. His was a profoundly thoughtful mind.

As he grew older and more independent, he established the pattern of spending the winters in Vienna in his simple three-room apartment. Always an early riser, and a man of rigid self-discipline, Brahms would prepare his morning coffee and get to work. What brightened his days were the twice-daily trips to the Red Hedgehog Inn where he ate his meals in the congenial company of musical and artistic friends.

To Brahms, travel and the enjoyment of nature were a necessity of life. In the springtime he loved to travel in Italy and to bathe in beauty. He enjoyed a good table too. Brahms received lasting inspiration from Italian art. One hears the Italian influence in the balanced serenity of his Piano Concerto No. 2. Brahms' summers were nearly always spent in the country. Like Beethoven, he was an outdoor person who received much inspiration on long walks. He loved Italy and Switzerland.

Traveling was no burden for Brahms as it is for some people. His method of packing for a journey was to pile all his clothes upon a table, then tilt it so that everything tumbled helter-skelter into the open trunk! Brahms never liked to write letters when on a trip, so he used postcards for a large part of his correspondence. Once he wrote a card containing two brief lines saying that there was a 16-page letter to follow. Naturally it never was written. Brahms had the heart of a child, and he especially loved children and pets. He enjoyed playing with toy soldiers which gave him musical ideas. One of Brahms' favorite books, even as an adult, was *Robinson Crusoe*.

The famous "war" between Brahms, the Classicist, and three other composers, Wagner, Bruckner, and Wolf, was stirred up mainly by the critics, in particular, Eduard Hanslick. When Brahms sent flowers to the funeral of Wagner in Venice, Wagner's wife, Cosima, sent them back.

Brahms began as a true Romantic composer, but in his mature works he succeeded in fusing opposing trends and wrote expressive yet concise music structurally rooted in the past. In a period that emphasized revolution in art, he held to the great musical traditions. His music shows the Classical influence of Bach, Handel, Haydn, and Beethoven, but his compositions are not mere imitations. He used the old forms so skillfully that they are filled with an entirely new spirit.

He never worried unduly about originality, believing that workmanship was fully as important as invention. Brahms said, "It is not hard to compose, . . . but it is hard to let the superfluous notes fall under the table." He was highly critical of his own work and destroyed many superfluous notes, thus producing a consistent high quality in his compositions.

Brahms, a true Classicist among the Romantics, never composed an opera, although he considered it at various times. Rather he chose to develop the forms of Beethoven's period. He was interested in Hungarian music, and used many folk song tunes in his compositions. In 1869 his Hungarian Dances met with phenomenal success, and they were played all over the world.

Brahms was one of the great song writers of the 19th century, and the song occupies a central position in his art. Schubert was his model for song writing. Brahms also composed many notable pieces for piano solos. His piano waltzes are delicious little masterpieces. Brahms was a great admirer of the Viennese waltzes of Johann Strauss.

In 1873 Brahms wrote the masterly Variations on a Theme by Haydn. This was followed by his four magnificent symphonies, called the "Indian Summer of the Symphony." They sometimes suffer from sluggish orchestration and a feeling of heaviness. Brahms also was the giant among composers of chamber music in the Romantic period. His Piano Quintet in F Minor and the profound

Clarinet Quintet are among his contributions to good listening. Brahms showed notable rhythmic originality, often using conflicting rhythms. He was a true musical scholar and he always continued his reading in literature and history.

Clara Schumann wrote to a friend telling about a symphony he was hoping to write, "Brahms is in good spirits, delighted with his summer holiday, and has a new Symphony in D Major ready in his head; the first movement he has put on paper." Brahms must have absorbed much sunshine and fresh air, as the mood of the second movement is bright and cheerful.

Brahms completed the soul-stirring *German Requiem* in 1868—he had been working on it since 1857. He directed the first performance on Good Friday. It met with success and Brahms moved into the front rank of German composers. News of his mother's death reached him in Vienna February 1, 1865. A friend found him at his piano weeping while playing Bach's Goldberg Variations. The incident recalls Beethoven's and Tchaikovsky's use of the "music cure" in times of special need.

Brahms' *Requiem* is a fundamentally Protestant one. Not only does it depart from the Latin and the well-known movements of the Catholic requiem mass, but its spirit is totally different. The heart of the Catholic requiem mass is the "Dies Irae" (Day of Wrath) or the last judgment which threatens the departed with purgatory or the pains of hell.

The *Requiem* by Brahms professes faith in the resurrection and reunion with God through the atoning death of Jesus Christ. The choice of words for the *Requiem* reveals an understanding of the vanity and emptiness of life when it is lived apart from knowing the consolation of Christian truth. The *Requiem* was partly motivated by the death of his mother and Schumann, especially the fifth movement. Brahms' music, like that of Schütz, Handel, and Bach is inspired by a deep concern with man's mortal life and his hope of heaven.

It was at school that the Bible first came into his hands, and as he matured he gained in knowledge of the Scriptures. He was a great admirer of Luther's translation of the Bible. Brahms said once, "In my study I can lay my hand on my Bible even in the dark."

The final illness of Clara Schumann resulted in Brahm's "Four Serious Songs." They were the supreme achievement of his last years. A few months after Clara's death, Brahms died of cancer. His death was hastened by his catching a chill at Clara Schumann's funeral. The Scripture text of the last movement of the *German Requiem* was read at Brahms' funeral. "Blessed are the dead which die in the Lord from henceforth: Yea, saith the Spirit, that they may rest from their labors; and their works do follow them" (Revelation 14:13).

Speaking of two influences that decidedly shaped Brahm's music, Niemann says, "The fact that Brahms began his creative activity with the German folk song and closed with the Bible reveals better than anything else the true religious creed of this great man of the people."

Brahms' last works were the 11 Chorale Preludes for organ. The last of these is entitled, "O World, I Must Depart From Thee." Brahms was buried in Vienna near the graves of Beethoven, Schubert, and Mozart. He was one of the few major composers whose greatness was recognized in his lifetime.

Recommended Reading

Geiringer, Karl. *Brahms: His Life and Work.* New York: Oxford University Press, 1947.

Niemann, Walter. *Brahms.* New York: Alfred A. Knopf, 1941.

Recommended Listening

Academic Festival Overture
Alto Rhapsody
Concerto No. 2 B Flat for piano
Concerto in D for violin
Four Serious Songs
German Requiem
Piano Music, Op. 116, 117, 118, 119
Quintet in F Minor for piano and strings
Songs—Wiegenlied, Von Ewige Liebe, etc.
4 Symphonies
Variations and Fugue on a Theme by Handel
Variations on a Theme by Haydn
Waltzes, Op. 39

Chapter XIII
Peter Ilyich Tchaikovsky
(1840—1893)

"Truly there would be reason to go mad were it not for music."—Tchaikovsky

Tchaikovsky, though not a concert pianist, wrote one of the most brilliant of concertos, the Piano Concerto in B Flat. He dedicated it to his friend, Nicholas Rubinstein, who told him it was impossible to play. Tchaikovsky was not convinced. He changed the dedication and gave the concerto to the German pianist and conductor, Hans von Bülow, who, not daring to present it in Europe, played it successfully for the first time in Boston. With Tchaikovsky's mastery of orchestral effect, rhythmic vitality, flair for the dramatic, and largeness of gesture, the Piano Concerto in B Flat is rightly a very popular work and is played often. It is a pageant of wonderful melodies, and Tchaikovsky's first masterpiece.

Peter Ilyich Tchaikovsky was born on May 7, 1840 in Votkinsk, Russia, but where he came from, musically speaking, is a mystery. He picked up a smattering of musical knowledge as a boy along with his brothers and sisters, but he was never suspected of possessing any special musical talent, and there had been no traces in his family. He studied to be a lawyer, and later worked as a clerk in the ministry of justice; but finally his creative talent was clearly revealed, and hearing the music of Mozart's *Don Giovanni* helped him make the decision to devote his life to music.

At the age of 23 he entered the newly founded Conservatory of St. Petersburg which was begun by Anton Rubinstein. Tchaikovsky was the first Russian to receive systematic training in music fundamentals. Working intensely hard, he completed the course in three years. He was then recommended by Rubinstein for a teaching position at the Conservatory of Moscow in 1866, and about that same time he began to compose seriously. He remained there for twelve years as a professor of harmony. He was highly regarded as a teacher, and despite the long hours and hard work, he continued to compose.

Tchaikovsky's melancholy and introspective temperament was clearly reflected in his music. He loved his mother with all the ardor of an acutely sensitive boy, and when she died of cholera when he was 14, his emotions were deeply affected. To alleviate the distress caused him both by the sudden death of his mother and his easygoing father's seeming indifference to it, Tchaikovsky composed a short waltz. Escaping into music when overwhelmed became a pattern in his life. He wrote some of his most lighthearted ballets in times of mental anguish.

Tchaikovsky's life was founded on raw nerves and abnormal sexual instincts. He was a homosexual and was tormented because of it. He also suffered from epilepsy, migraine headaches, insomnia, and attacks of depression. His life contained all the elements of tragedy, and yet he continued to produce music with unchecked ardor, and he lived a life of ever-increasing artistic achievement. In their biography *Beloved Friend,* Bowen and Meck include this excerpt from one of Tchaikovsky's letters:"I have some very low moments, but an insatiable thirst for work consoles me. . . . If one lacks the right mood, one must force oneself to work, otherwise nothing will be accomplished." Another time he wrote, "Without work, life has no meaning for me." He was a very humble man who rarely believed in the excellence of his work.

While still teaching at the Conservatory in Moscow, Tchaikovsky at the age of 29 composed his fantasy *Romeo and Juliet*. It is one of his finest works and marks the beginning of his career. Considering how late Tchaikovsky came to the serious study of music, the quickness of his technical development is amazing. He greatly admired Shakespeare and Dickens, especially *Pickwick Papers*. Tchaikovsky found great pleasure in literature and the theater. The form of *Romeo and Juliet* is similar to Mendelssohn's overture, *A Midsummer-Night's Dream*. *Romeo and Juliet* was received coldly at first, but now the work is an international favorite. In it we hear some of his great melodies, particularly the lovers' theme, his ripe harmonies, and vigorous rhythms.

For his mature, masterly piece, *Francesca Da Rimini*, Tchaikovsky chose a subject from Dante's *Divine Comedy*. The story is of the love of Francesca and Paolo who Dante places in the Inferno where they are seen as two lost souls wandering disconsolately. It is expressed musically by Tchaikovsky with deep sensitivity and compassion.

Hoping for stability in his life, at the age of 37 Tchaikovsky married Antonina, one of the students at the Moscow Conservatory. She had cunningly pursued him and the marriage was a disaster. She was an unsavory person and ended her days in a mental institution. Close to a nervous breakdown, Tchaikovsky attempted suicide. At this moment of desperate need, Madame Nadejda von Meck, a wealthy widow with 11 children, who had already heard some of Tchaikovsky's music and was deeply moved by the beauty and sensitivity of it, commissioned him to write other works.

In 1877 this took the more substantial shape of an annual allowance to free him so he could compose. The immediate result of her patronage was Tchaikovsky's Fourth Symphony. Madame von Meck was passionately musical in the Russian manner where one loses oneself completely in sound. (For a while she had Claude Debussy in her palatial home to instruct her children in music.)

Thus began an extraordinary correspondence between the two which lasted 13 years and has served as the principal source for biographies of Tchaikovsky. *Beloved Friend,* an excellent book about Tchaikovsky, includes these interesting letters. The 19th century was a great time of letter writing. Tchaikovsky was a compulsive correspondent. He also kept a diary, some of which he destroyed. Madame von Meck and Tchaikovsky mutually agreed never to meet, yet the love between them was profound. He respected her for understanding his need for privacy and solitude. Through their correspondence and the gifts of money, she gave him the encouragement and confidence he desperately needed. It is one of the most celebrated friendships in history, but it ended tragically.

Throughout his life Tchaikovsky was obsessed with the idea that he was fighting a battle against fate. In his Fourth Symphony, dedicated to Madame von Meck and one of his finest works, we encounter the fatalism that reflects the pessimism of both of them. Russia is a land of sorrow and tragedy which is reflected in its literature and music. Tchaikovsky, like many Russians, habitually drank too much as a temporary escape from an oppressive world, but he was certainly not an alcoholic. He was a sensitive, highstrung individual easily depressed about his life and work.

Tchaikovsky laid great weight on the Russian element in his music. Stravinsky said, "Tchaikovsky is the most Rus-

sian of us all." Michael Glinka, who wrote operas in the
early 1800's, is considered the father of serious Russian
music. After his death, his sister lived for 50 years spread-
ing propaganda for his music. Her home became a salon
for "The Five"—Balakirev, Cui, Rimsky-Korsakov, Borodin, and Mussorgsky, who were contemporary with
Tchaikovsky. They were all amateurs except their leader,
Balakirev. Balakirev urged Tchaikovsky to write *Romeo
and Juliet,* but later accused him of being too much an
admirer of Western culture.

Like Dvorak and several other composers, Tchaikovsky
had a great love of nature and his native soil. In 1885 he
bought his own house in the vicinity of Moscow after many
years of a roaming life. Here he lived until the year before
his death when he moved to the nearby town of Klin. It is
known today as the Tchaikovsky House Museum. Ever a
generous man, when he heard there was no school for
children in the village, he promptly gave money to establish one. Tchaikovsky was deeply patriotic, although he
was ashamed of the contrasts of life in Russia, and of the
injustices of which the czarist government was guilty.

Once Madame von Meck freed him from teaching, he
formed the habits of work which remained with him for
the rest of his life. Even when traveling he tried, not always
successfully, to follow the same routine. From 8 to 9 in the
morning he would drink tea and read his Bible. Then he
would work. Later in the afternoon, he would walk. Having read someplace that in order to keep healthy, a person
should walk for two hours a day, this he did with scrupul-
ousness. It was on the walks, many times, that the work of
composition was initiated, ideas tried and jotted down in
little notebooks. He felt strongly that an artist must not
give in to that powerful human trait of laziness. Like most
artists Tchaikovsky craved solitude, so his ideas would not
be stolen from him in breezy, indifferent conversation.

Tchaikovsky dedicated The Serenade for Strings to

Madame von Meck. In the first movement he attempted to adopt the style of Mozart, who was his favorite composer. The second movement exemplifies his marvelous gift for melody. As one critic said, "There is always a waltz in his music." The second movement is actually a *valse triste* and brings to mind the 19th century salon with its superficial gaiety tinged with melancholy.

Like many artists and musicians Tchaikovsky loved Venice and Florence. He also spent time in Switzerland in the village of Clarens near Montreux. As one walks along the lake stopping now and then to look at the mountains and flowers, and to feed the swans, it is easy to picture Tchaikovsky having done the same. He was always composing, even when traveling about to conduct his music. When Carnegie Hall was built, Tchaikovsky was invited to conduct in New York City and was a resounding success. His great personal charm and handsome appearance won him friends in many countries. Saint-Saëns said, "He was the gentlest and kindest of men."

The music of Tchaikovsky is a mixture of folk melody, cosmopolitan Italian opera, French ballet, and German symphony, but still very Russian. His immense popularity is due to tunefulness and beautiful melodies that sweep over one like a wave, and also his brilliant orchestration. He was one of the finest orchestrators of all time, and Tchaikovsky is at his best in the ballets. Even his symphonies have ballet-like touches. Lack of form, so apparent in his early symphonies, was his worst musical defect. Tchaikovsky was the first Russian composer to gain international fame.

The home of his sister, Alexandra, and her husband and children, provided a place of stability and comfort for Tchaikovsky. Tchaikovsky had a genuine affection for children. His first ballet, *Swan Lake,* was originally planned as entertainment for his nieces and nephews. Yet always underneath, this gentle man was lonely and frustrated. He said, "Regretting the past and hoping for the future without ever being satisfied with the present—this is how my life is spent."

His three ballets have become classics. In *Swan Lake* (1875-1876) Tchaikovsky strove for a simple fairy-tale style combined with theatrical brilliance to meet the needs of the classical Russian ballet. His superb orchestral technique and delicacy of touch make it a masterpiece.

In 1888 and 1889 he wrote *Sleeping Beauty*. The waltz in it, which is rightly famous, has a melodious, lyrical style. Some of the most delightful music he ever wrote is in *Sleeping Beauty*. Tchaikovsky was passionately fond of the waltz all his life. It was his way to escape from the troubling reality of life into the lovely, but artificial, world of ballet and music.

Three years after *Sleeping Beauty*, Tchaikovsky wrote *The Nutcracker Suite*. It is a Christmas Eve ballet about a little girl who dreams that the nutcracker she received as a present has turned into a handsome prince. In the "Dance of the Flowers" we find the modern orchestra in full color and Tchaikovsky at his best.

One can see clearly how he found consolation from his personal sorrows through writing charming, cheerful music, because shortly before he wrote *The Nutcracker Suite*, Madame von Meck, in a cruel and unexpected manner, broke their friendship. Her favorite son became desperately ill, and she imagined that she had neglected him by showing so much attention to Tchaikovsky. Another biographer explained that she discontinued the allowance imagining herself to be financially ruined, which apparently was pure delusion. By then Tchaikovsky no longer really needed the money, but he was deeply wounded by the way she terminated their friendship. Within a few months he became an old man. He never got over the shock, and on his deathbed three years later he called over and over for Madame von Meck. She died soon after he did.

Madame von Meck was a strong atheist, an intense and dominating woman. She was proud of her independence of God and society and often chided Tchaikovsky for longing to feel the Christian truths more strongly and to have a more secure faith. In their biography of Tchaiskovsky, Bowen and Meck include this revealing excerpt from one letter Tchaikovsky wrote to Madame von Meck: "On one side my mind refuses to be convinced by dogma . . . on the other hand, my education, and the ingrained habits of childhood, combined with the story of Christ and his teaching, all persuade me, in spite of myself, to turn to Him with prayers when I am sad, with gratitude when I am happy."

Tchaikovsky wrote eight operas, but only *Eugene Onegin* and *The Queen of Spades* are now regularly performed. *Eugene Onegin,* with its famous letter scene in Act I, was only a token success at its Moscow première, but enjoyed great popularity in St. Petersburg, because of the Czar's admiration. His Violin Concerto is one of the most popular as well as one of the best. Of his songs, "None But The Lonely Heart" is best known. Of prime importance are Tchaikovsky's last three symphonies. They are rich in content, tension, and melody. His love of percussion instruments is noteworthy.

Concerning the Sixth Symphony, Tchaikovsky said, "I have put my whole soul into this work." He wrote it after the shattering break with Madame von Meck. Again Tchaikovsky, taking refuge from the sorrows of life, wrote his finest music. With his Sixth Symphony the 19th century is completed—from the optimism and triumphant finale of Beethoven's symphonies to the twilight anguish of Tchaikovsky's last musical statement. His brother, Modeste, gave it the name, *Pathetique.*

After completing his last symphony, he went to St. Petersburg to conduct it, but the public did not appreciate it. This great symphony had a cold and indifferent reception, but the verdict was speedily reversed—too late for Tchaikovsky who, like his mother earlier, died of cholera. He was 53. The Sixth Symphony is one of the most popular of the 19th century with sweeping climaxes and tragic beauty. The music of Tchaikovsky with all its strength and beauty nevertheless expressed the pessimism that attended the final phase of the Romantic movement.

Recommended Reading

Bowen, Catherine Drinker, and von Meck, Barbara. *Beloved Friend: The Story of Tchaikovsky and Nadejda von Meck.* New York: Dover Publications, 1946.

Warrack, John. *Tchaikovsky.* London: Haish Hamilton, 1973.

Recommended Listening

Capriccio Italien
Concerto B Flat Minor—Piano and orchestra
Concerto D Major—Violin and orchestra
Eugene Onegin–Selections
Francesca da Rimini
Marche Slave
Nutchacker Suite
1812 Overture
Romeo and Juliet
Serenade in C for Strings
Sleeping Beauty Ballet
Swan Lake Ballet
Symphony No. 4
Symphony No. 5
Symphony No. 6—*Pathetique*

Chapter XIV

Anton Dvorak
(1841—1904)

"His music expresses joy in life, love of man and nature, faith in God, and devotion to his country."—Robertson

Czechoslovakia is surrounded by Russia, Poland, Germany, Austria, Hungary, and Russian soldiers. It was cold and damp when we flew into Prague recently. The weather seemed to reflect the downcast spirit of the Czechs as they watch their beautiful city slowly crumbling into ruin. As we walked in the Old Town Square and circled the John Huss statue and watched the figures turn on the old clock, it appeared upon first glance that they were about to restore some of the ancient buildings, but on closer examination "restoration" is actually outright neglect or total abandon. It is one way the people fight against the Russian occupation, by deliberately being poor workmen. One Czech explained, "Our national disaster is occupation. Perhaps, therefore, our greatest quality is patience."

Another characteristic of the Czechs is their love of music and dancing. "We have none of Dostoyevsky in us," this man explained. "It is better to laugh than weep." This has been true of the Czechs down through history. No matter what nation dominated them the saving factor for the future of Czech music and dance was that the country people remained obstinately Czech, and they kept in their hands a torch by which Smetana and, after him, Dvorak, lighted fires that the whole world could see. Today in communist-controlled Czechoslovakia Dvorak enjoys great popularity as his music, not the present enslavement, represents the people's true spirit.

Burney writing in 1772 spoke of the Czechs as the most musical people in all Europe. He noticed in one of his tours that in the villages boys and girls are taught music in the schools. He saw them playing the violin, oboe, and bassoon, and little children industriously practicing on four clavichords owned by the school master.

In such a village Anton Dvorak was born on September 8, 1841. His father was the local butcher and innkeeper of Nelahozeves in Bohemia, a small village which lies on the banks of the River Moldau about 45 miles north of Prague. At the door of his father's inn young Anton first appeared as a musician, taking his place among the fiddlers who were there to play for the spontaneous dancing in the streets during a national festival.

Anton Dvorak was the eldest son, and though they were a poor family struggling for the bare means of existence, he grew up healthy and high-spirited. At an early age he showed his love for music. The village teacher taught him to sing and play the violin and organ. Dvorak truly thirsted for musical knowledge. When he was 12, his father sent him to nearby Zlonic where he went to school. There he made friends with the organist and chief musician in town who instructed the boy in theory, organ, and pianoforte. His teacher admitted that Dvorak was "extraordinarily full of promise," but in spite of it Dvorak's father ordered him to come home and learn to be a butcher.

Dvorak tried to obey his father, but it was a depressing, terrible time in his life. Finally the 16-year-old Dvorak was allowed to go to Prague and attend the Organ School. He lodged for awhile with a cousin who was married to a tailor. Dvorak was not happy there. It is possible that his relatives looked down on him. The boy was a peasant, not very sociable, a quiet person, and his only interest in life was music to which he was completely dedicated. His early years were beset with difficulties. He had to support himself by playing the violin and viola in cafés and theaters, and the organ in church.

For awhile he lived with another relative, but there was no piano. A friend by the name of Anger who played with him in the theater orchestra invited Dvorak to share his room. Anger said that he had an old spinet that Dvorak could use for composing. The instrument was in the bedroom where, besides the congenial Anger, there lived also a medical student interested in opera, two other students, and a tourist guide. Needless to say, the arrangement did not last long.

Anton Dvorak, always silent and reserved, once grimly declared that in his early days in Prague he always had enough paper to make a fire. What he meant was that he used his early compositions to begin the fire in his stove. In the 12 years after he left the Organ School, and until his emergence before the public as a composer in 1871, Dvorak spent hours each day studying other composers, particularly Beethoven, and then writing and writing music, which he soon destroyed. "If I ought, I can" might well have been the motto of Dvorak, and he had a firm, inner conviction that he would eventually succeed as a composer. Dvorak was a hard worker and determined to overcome.

Robertson says that between 1863 and 1869 his burnings were on so large a scale that he must rarely have been cold. But he continued to compose, steadily cherishing an obstinate faith in himself. All through his life he refused to send to the printer music which did not satisfy his own critical standard.

In 1873 Dvorak married Anna, a good contralto singer and she became a practical, energetic wife. Though they were poor, his home now formed a center in which he could create new works in peace. His was an unusually happy family life. The noises in the home did not worry him at all. His favorite spot for work was the kitchen, where at a small table he sketched out his symphonies and other compositions amid the usual clutter of pots and pans. Steeped in domestic happiness Dvorak penetrated deeper and deeper to the roots of his own individuality. Finally freeing himself from copying other composers, he now discovered that in his own soul there was music from his rural Czech background.

The artistic life of the Czech nation was given a great boost in 1860 when Italy's victories over Austria brought about a larger degree of political freedom in Czechoslovakia. Smetana, who is called the "Father of Czech music" (1824-1884), returned from exile in Sweden and helped to found the "Society of Arts." He also became the conductor of the Czech National Theater Orchestra in which Dvorak played the viola. Smetana intended to provide the theater with a repertory of native works. Casting about for ideas of what he could write, he decided that the best platform for propagating the national idea in music was the opera as it appeals to both the eye and ear.

So Smetana wrote his jolly, spirited *The Bartered Bride,* and it eventually brought him worldwide fame, but more immediately, the Prague citizens, "to whom music was as catching as measles," took to their hearts the popular airs by one of their own countrymen. Also notable is Smetana's symphonic poem series *My Fatherland.*

The Bartered Bride is a flawless work of comic art, and of course, Dvorak was present in the orchestra pit at all rehearsals and performances; he too caught the "disease" of opera. Anger said that in this period Dvorak frequently and gladly accompanied him to hear Wagner's operas, and finally, in 1874 Dvorak produced his own opera. But it was not a success. Nothing daunted, the overcomer Dvorak rewrote the opera in three months. His perseverance was rewarded, and soon his operas began to bring him national acclaim. By 1876, Dvorak was able to give up his various ways of earning a living and devote himself entirely to composition.

One of the first compositions Dvorak wrote which brought him into notice as a composer of merit was a patriotic cantata. His rise to prominence dates from this successful performance. Around the same time the already famous Brahms came upon certain duets of Dvorak, and particularly appreciating the freshness and naturalness of his music with the Bohemian flavor recommended Dvorak for an annual pension. Brahms became a good friend of Dvorak and remembering himself how appreciative he was of Robert Schumann's help before he had published any music, Brahms introduced Dvorak to his publisher, Simrock. Simrock liked the music and printed the charming *Moravian Duets* in 1876.

Following on this success came a commission in 1877 for a series of Slavonic Dances. When published, this cycle of sparkling, lively pieces swept Europe and established Dvorak's world fame. They also stirred interest in Czechoslovakian music. Dvorak in commenting on Brahms in a letter said, "What a warm heart and great spirit there is in that man."

A performance of the Slavonic Dances in London in 1879 made Dvorak known to British music lovers, and he went many times to England to conduct his music. Especially well received was his *Stabat Mater,* written in memory of the death of his oldest daughter. It is the noblest manifestation of Dvorak's religious inspiration.

Dvorak continued to write chamber music, symphonies, operas, and songs. His most famous in the last group is "Songs My Mother Taught Me." It is a near perfect little work of art ending with a phrase of unforgettable beauty. The operas, though popular at the time, have failed to enjoy lasting success, although *Rusalka* is the best-loved of his stage works. In 1883 Dvorak wrote the brilliant Hussite Overture, a powerfully built work based on the chorale "St. Wenceslaus" and the Hussite hymn "All Ye Who are Warriors of God."

It should be remembered that the national hero of Czechoslovakia is John Huss (ca. 1369-1415). He was a priest and professor of philosophy at the University of Prague, and a man of high moral character and life. Huss was an outstanding preacher and very popular with the people, because he spoke out clearly and fearlessly against ecclesiastical greed and corruption. Huss was "a reformer before the Reformation," strongly influenced by John Wycliffe. He insisted that the Holy Scriptures are the only rule in matters of life and religion. Following his excommunication, the whole nation rallied around him, but the enemy was stronger. After being deceived and cruelly tortured, John Huss was burned at the stake in 1415. As he was dying he sang, "Jesus Christ the Son of the Living God, have mercy on me." Under King Wenceslaus, the Czech Reformation began in 1424. This resulted in the Hussite Wars in which the blind general John Zizka led the Czechs against the Catholics and Germans and conquered Prague.

In 1890 Dvorak enjoyed a personal triumph in Moscow where two concerts were arranged for him by another composer friend, Tchaikovsky. Then in 1892 Dvorak accepted the post of director of the newly established National Conservatory of Music in New York. It was started by Mrs. Jeannette M. Thurber, an enthusiastic music lover and wife of a wealthy grocery magnate. It was not easy for

Dvorak to leave his beloved Bohemia and go to New York City, but accompanied by his wife and two of their numerous children, he accepted the position.

Now a famous man, Dvorak was still basically a conservative, quiet son of the soil, not very sociable and rather suspicious, preferring to keep within a narrow circle. He proved to be a fine teacher but an indifferent administrator because he turned down the social invitations showered on him. He had work to do and he needed to go to bed early in order to do it. One of his delights in New York was to go to the railway stations and watch the trains thunder by or to Central Park and listen to the birds which reminded him of home.

It has been said that the harvest of Dvorak's American visit is not rich numerically, but it may be compared to a full harvest of the purest and heaviest corn without chaff. Dvorak's talent for composition was of the highest order, and in his Symphony No. 9 in E Minor, *From the New World,* he seemed to please everyone. There are few notable works of permanent value that have been immediately accepted and appreciated by the public at large, but the *New World Symphony* is one of them.

Most of the orchestration for the symphony was done in Spillville, Iowa, where the composer went in the summertime. Dvorak suffered badly from homesickness in New York, but in Spillville he found his own people. The small town was made up of a colony of Bohemian people from Czechoslovakia. There he could speak his native tongue, go to church, sing some of the sweet, sad songs from his homeland, play at the many festivals, and eat and drink among his people. Also in Spillville, he had his whole family together, the other four children having been sent for.

The *New World Symphony* is in the spirit of folk music, and the majority of the melodies are unmistakably Czech. Sweetness of sound is a chief characteristic of Dvorak's music. The largo of the Second Movement has a hauntingly beautiful melody played by the English horn. There is a sense of longing about it, and a spiritual has been adapted from it, "Going Home." One loves the melodic invention of Dvorak, his transparency, and heartwarming simplicity. His is happy music with a touch of sadness. The black singer, Henry Burleigh, studied with Dvorak at the Conservatory and introduced Dvorak to the beautiful songs of his race.

For a while there was a controversy whether Dvorak had used authentic American themes in his symphony. As Robertson shows, he settled it in a letter he wrote to the Berlin conductor, Nedbal: "Please omit the nonsense about my having made use of 'Indian' and 'American' themes—that is a lie. I merely tried to write in the spirit of these national melodies."

Also in America, Dvorak wrote his masterly Cello Concerto, the American String Quartet, Humoresque, and the Ten Biblical Songs. These are a fervent and intimate expression of Dvorak's deep piety. Today they are played often in Czechoslovakia, and it means something much deeper to the Christian people living there who not only yearn for political freedom but for freedom to worship the Living God.

After three years Dvorak returned to Prague—he was very homesick for his beautiful, little country. Success never spoiled him. He remained what he had been, a simple, rather obstinate, God-fearing man, most always silent and reserved, neither asking for advice nor receiving it. After the stunning success of the *New World Symphony* in New York, Boston, and Vienna, Dvorak commented simply, "May God be thanked."

Happiness for him lay in his family circle, and for the most part, in pleasures that money cannot buy. He spoke of his genius as "the gift of God" or "God's voice" speaking to him. After finishing a great work he was always afraid lest that voice might not be heard again and his creative faculty withdrawn. With Handel and Haydn, Dvorak's music was among the healthiest of all composers.

Dvorak caught a chill standing at the railway station in Prague on his regular visit to see the locomotives, and he died suddenly at the dinner table shortly afterwards on May 1, 1904. His music is the most inventive and spontaneously musical of all national composers. It is joyous and untouched by tedium, and continues to bring comfort, not only to the people of his beloved land, but to all nations. Anton Dvorak is one of the most human and lovable of the great composers.

Recommended Reading
Robertson, Alec. *Dvorak.* New York: Collier Books, 1962.

Recommended Listening
Ten Biblical Songs
Carnival Overture
Concerto in B Minor for Cello
Quartet in F, *American*
Slavonic Dances
Stabat Mater
Symphony No. 7 in D Minor
Symphony No. 8 in G
Symphony No. 9 in E Minor, *New World* Symphony
Trio in E Minor 'Dumky"
Smetana—
    Bartered Bride—Overture
    The Moldau (from: *My Fatherland*)

Chapter XV
Gustav Mahler
(1860—1911)

"Where do I go? I go wandering in the mountains, seeking rest for my lonely heart!"—"The Song of the Earth"

Bruno Walter in speaking about Gustav Mahler said that his spirit never knew escape from the torturing question, "For what?" Few people worked harder or accomplished more than Mahler, but he was rarely content. All his life was a conflict between belief and unbelief, and he was obsessed with the themes, death and the life beyond. Mahler was Jewish, and like many Austrian-Jewish intellectuals he became a convert to Roman Catholicism, but he remained the perpetual doubter all his life, yearning for the ecstasy of faith and the "wholeness of soul" that comes from certainty.

Gustav Mahler was born in Kalište, Bohemia, in 1860. Around the age of four, being fascinated by the band music he heard in the street near his father's inn (which was also the family home) and the folk music sung by the Czech people, he began writing his own pieces and trying them on the accordion. Later he found an old piano in the attic and gradually he learned to play it. His vocation was never doubted. By 15 he was so proficient musically that he was accepted as a student at the Vienna Conservatory and was thankful to leave the village of Iglau where he grew up. At the Conservatory he was a friend of Hugo Wolf, who later became one of the great song writers.

Mahler's father was an Austrian-Jewish tavern keeper, a cruel man of "fierce vitality." He was self-educated and resented his wife's social superiority. He mistreated her, and young Mahler's childhood was complicated by the quarrels between his parents and the illnesses and deaths among his 11 brothers and sisters. This may help to explain Mahler's obsession with death and his unceasing quest to discover some meaning in life. Mahler had such empathy with his fragile mother that he copied unconsciously her slight limp. As one friend commented, "He walked with a lopsided gait." Also he inherited his mother's weak heart. His father's brutality haunted the sensitive musician throughout his life. Add to that the racial tensions he had to endure, both in Bohemia and Vienna, and one sees he had a difficult beginning.

After getting his diploma from the Conservatory in Vienna, Mahler, a prodigious worker, supported himself by occasional teaching while trying to gain recognition as a composer. His poverty during these years was chronic, and reluctantly he decided for a career as an operatic conductor, since at that age he probably was unaware of his rare, almost uncanny talents in that direction. Finally, at the age of 20 he turned to conducting as a livelihood and set aside time in the summers for composing.

When his parents died in 1889, Mahler took on the responsibility of caring for his remaining brothers and sisters. In one of his illnesses Mahler went to Italy, and his sister, Justine, went along to care for him. Later she became his faithful housekeeper. The radiance of the Italian springtime helped to restore his health.

After 17 years of conducting in various European opera houses, Mahler rose to the top of his profession and was asked to be the musical director of the Imperial Opera House in Vienna in 1897. Though he became one of the greatest conductors of modern times, he was frustrated. He wanted most of all to be a composer.

The years Mahler spent in Vienna were brilliant because he was an eminent interpreter, especially of Wagner and Mozart. But the time was also discordant and strife-ridden. Mahler was a relentless conductor. His striving for perfection gained him the enmity of the performers, but the adulation of the audience. As one critic said, "Mahler, whose neuroses made Tchaikovsky's neuroses look healthy," was a tempestuous, restless, irritable, impatient personality who inevitably provoked storms wherever he went. His motives were never really mean but stemmed more from confusion, as his life was a tug-of-war. He longed for freedom to compose, but had to continue conducting in order to live. Invariably he carried a parcel of books and music under his arm. He was always intent on learning. Of Mahler's dedication to music there was no doubt.

Mahler easily made enemies with his intensity, arrogance, and insecurity dating back to his childhood. All his life he suffered from fearful headaches (which would explain some of his irritability), but he almost never cancelled a rehearsal or performance. Mahler had fanatical energy, ruthless zeal, and musical genius. Even though his health was poor, he was determined to overcome. He was a tireless swimmer and an indefatigable hiker. His appearance was that of a slim, yet well-muscled sportsman.

Mahler married Alma Schindler in 1902 after having had a long series of unhappy affairs. Much could be said about Alma. Books have been written about her, and she has written one herself. Although Mahler's love for Alma was genuine, it was a frustrating marriage for both of them. Mahler was 41 and Alma 23, and the conductor-composer (who lived for his music) could not devote himself exclusively to his beautiful, young wife. He said once, "I cannot do anything but work."

She was a brilliant pianist and gifted composer herself, and soon she became an accurate copyist of his scores and an understanding and sympathetic critic of his music. Alma introduced him to many artistic people with whom she was acquainted. With her originality of mind and strong ambition she was worthy to become the wife and companion of Mahler. Alma could be extravagantly generous and inordinately mean. As one person said, "If Mahler was selfish, Alma was more selfish still."

Gustav Mahler did most of his composing with frenzied speed in the summer between hectic seasons of conducting, and he would orchestrate his works during the winter in the morning before rehearsals. He was happiest when he was in his studio far away in the woods at Maiernigg, wearing his oldest clothes, walking and composing. The balcony of his studio-bedroom had a magnificent view over the lake. His music is filled with sounds of nature he must have heard there and in other places he worked during the summer.

Mahler spoke of himself as "the summer composer," and the great dream of his life was to earn enough money so he could retire when he was 50 and devote his entire time to composing. It was one of the reasons he drove himself relentlessly. It is surprising when one first considers it that Mahler turned to symphonies and songs for his creative expression because his life as a conductor centered in the opera house, but his autobiographical music was more effectively expressed in programmatic symphonies and songs.

The first years of Gustav and Alma's marriage were brightened by the birth of their two children and Mahler's increasing productivity as a composer. In 1904 he read some poems by the German poet, Friedrich Rückert, lamenting the death of his children. The tragedy so affected Rückert, he poured out his sorrow in countless poems. When Mahler began to write the beautiful and heartrending music known today as the *Kindertotenlieder* (Songs on the Death of Children), Alma declared that she found his choice of such a sad text "incomprehensible." "For heaven's sake," she said, "don't tempt Providence."

When three years later their beloved Maria died of diphtheria and scarlet fever at the age of five, Mahler was inconsolable. Even though he had many character faults and was egotistical, there was in his personality a childlike simplicity and idealism which made his suffering unbearable. The *Kindertotenlieder* is one of Mahler's most intimate and profoundly moving compositions.

Mahler's Sixth Symphony reveals a superstitious element in his personality. In the finale there are three climactic hammer blows which represent the three blows of fate which fall on the hero. In 1907 Mahler identified the three blows of fate with his own life:

(1) His resignation from the Vienna Opera House. (After Mahler came under a venomous attack in the press in 1907, he asked for his discharge.)

(2) The death of his daughter, Maria.

(3) The diagnosis of his fatal heart disease by a doctor.

Mahler was told that his whole way of life would have to change and that his favorite long walks would have to be given up. It was a time of dejection, but Mahler was not yet through. Music was his only way of life, and so he went on a concert tour to St. Petersburg and Helsinki. Then he accepted an invitation to conduct Mozart and Wagner at the Metropolitan Opera House in New York, and he and Alma crossed the Atlantic for the first time in December, 1907. Upon arriving in New York, Alma said, "We were so excited that we forgot our cares."

Mahler's last three years were spent in New York City where he was invited to conduct both the Metropolitan Opera and the New York Philharmonic Orchestra. Summers were devoted to composing and conducting in Europe. From the proceeds of his American engagements he started to build a home in Austria where he could retire and compose in peace, but this dream was never realized. Toward the end of his life a crisis in his marriage, in addition to the perpetual inner doubts, persuaded Mahler to consult Sigmund Freud. But he found no spiritual help, and the meaning of life for him remained as obscure as ever.

In 1911, now a very sick man, Mahler returned to Europe, and after a brief time in Paris, he was brought back to Vienna. He died there at the age of 50. His last words were, "Mozart . . . Mozart." Gustav Mahler was buried next to his daughter, Maria, in Grinzing near Vienna.

The music of Mahler was not always well received. After the premiere of the Third Symphony in Germany in 1902, a reviewer concluded that "the composer should be shot." When Mahler first performed the Fourth Symphony in Vienna, it drove the audience to such fury that fist fights broke out all over the concert hall. When he met with such incomprehension and lack of appreciation, he said obstinately, "My time will come!" And Mahler's time has come. As one of our recent conductors has said, "Mahler was a high-strung genius who speaks today to a high-strung generation."

Mahler is an important forerunner of 20th century techniques of composition. Such widely differing composers as Schönberg, Berio, Shostakovich, and Britten have acknowledged his influence. He was a profound admirer of Wagner, in whose music we find the culmination of the Romantic agony. Mahler was the last in a great line of Viennese symphonists which included Haydn, Mozart,

Beethoven, Schubert, Brahms, and Bruckner. One could say that Wagner was the door and Mahler, the last of the diatonic composers, opened it to Schönberg and 20th century music.

Mahler spoke of himself "as a pupil of Bruckner." Although he probably never actually studied with him, Mahler was the devoted disciple of Anton Bruckner, yet without his religious beliefs.

Bruckner was a solitary, simple, and devout soul. His religion was the foundation of everything he did. He even introduced masses into his symphonies. Bruckner was born of a poor family in Upper Austria. He was a fine organist, and at first expressed himself in church music. He was a humble man, never at home among the intellectuals in Vienna. He dedicated his Ninth Symphony "to the good Lord." His was a medieval soul living in the 19th century struggling with the problems of how to find an artistic relationship to God. When Mahler used a chorale tune in his Fifth Symphony, his wife said, "Bruckner yes, but not you."

The compositions of Mahler consist of nine symphonies (a tenth unfinished), some songs, and four song cycles somewhat in the manner of Schubert and Schumann. He wrote nothing for the stage in spite of his vast experience conducting operas. His symphonies are long, programmatic (like Richard Strauss') and demand enormous performing resources. "To write a symphony," Mahler said, "is, for me, to construct a world." He conducted 1,000 performers in the première of his Eighth Symphony. Today it is referred to as the *Symphony of a Thousand.*

Lyricism is the essential ingredient of Mahler's music. The melody is long of line with intermittent extravagant leaps which help to heighten the power to communicate intense emotion (Schönberg also used this technique). One finds in the music of Mahler great beauty and power along with banality and even vulgarity. Mahler was a pioneer of brilliant orchestration with a unique sense of color.

The main themes of Mahler are typically romantic, the beauty of nature (he said once, "My music is, throughout and always, but a sound of nature"), love and faith, destiny and death. His music is full of unrest and nostalgia. He usually ended a symphony in a different key than he began it, and he has the Schubertian wavering between major and minor. Even in his music Mahler was never satisfied, constantly making revisions. He was one of the most adventurous and fastidious of composers in his treatment of instrumental combinations. In spite of massive orchestras he maintained clarity of line and lightness of texture. Mahler's style is based on orchestral counterpoint. He was a master of technique.

Mahler required many unusual instruments—harness bells, mandolin, guitar, glockenspiel, and harmonium— and employed a variety of original percussion instruments including a hammer. Mahler was fascinated with band music, and his symphonies resound with the sound of drums and horns. His use of foreign elements in his symphonies has been ascribed to lack of originality, but more correctly it is a specifically modern approach. Stockhausen has said that what Mahler did was to integrate all the elements, from the most banal and commonplace, into a whole which transcends them. Mahler used intruments in their extreme range and had some instruments offstage to achieve a sense of distance. His music has flashes of haunting beauty which speak to questing, doubting souls.

Let us now turn briefly to several of his symphonies. The introduction to the First Symphony represents the awakening of nature at early dawn to spring without end. One of the important motifs is the cuckoo call.

The second movement is a scherzo-waltz-ländler so typical of Viennese music. Mahler had absorbed much of Austrian popular song and dance.

The third movement is an ironic funeral march with the simple French children's song, "Frère Jacques." A funeral march was one of Mahler's favorite symbols and it expressed his obsession with death. Most all of his symphonies have marches. He also used chorales to create the atmosphere of religious faith.

In Mahler's first four symphonies he gave out detailed programs. Words were important in his creative process. Later he suppressed these when the critics accused him of not being able to write absolute music. In the First, Second, Third, and Fourth Symphonies Mahler used music from his *Wunderhorn* cycle *(Youth's Magic Horn)*. These symphonies, like Beethoven's Ninth, employ the human voice.

The Second Symphony is his famous *Resurrection*. In Mahler's own program notes are the following observations: "I have called the first movement 'funeral rites' . . . it is the hero from my Symphony No. 1 whom I am laying in his grave. And the question asked of him is, 'To what purpose have you lived? What next? What is life and what is death? Is it all a hollow dream?' "

Second movement—"Remembering the past . . . a ray of sunshine, pure and unspoiled, from the hero's life."

Third movement—"When you awaken from the wistful dream of the second movement . . . life appears senseless . . . and like a dreadful nightmare."

Fourth movement—"The stirring voice of simple faith reaches our ear; I am of God and will go back to God."

Fifth movement—"The voice in the desert sounds: the end of all life has come . . . The earth trembles, the graves are opening, the dead rise and march past in endless procession. The great and the small of this earth—kings and beggars . . . the trumpets call—in the midst of a horrible silence we seem to hear a distant nightingale . . . a choir of saints sing, 'Resurrection'—And the glory of God appears . . . and lo and behold! There is no judgment . . . An overwhelming Love shines. We know and are."

While Mahler was a great composer and conductor and his music beautiful, it is nevertheless foolish to get one's doctrine from someone who never found peace in his life. What Mahler is expressing in the Second Symphony is humanism and high Romanticism and certainly not the truth expressed in the Scriptures. There will indeed be a final judgment, and Christ himself will be the Judge. There will be condemnation for those who have rejected the Savior and forgiveness for all who have believed in Him during this life.

In the Eighth Symphony Mahler reverts to the programmatic and philosophically motivated symphonies of his early period. Mahler had the idea of an infinite, cosmic music. But unable to understand the infinite, personal God as revealed to us in Christ Jesus, he leaped into a mystical, irrational, and humanistic religion which ends in emptiness and despair. Mahler strove for the monumental, but he flounders in this gigantic work.

One is aware that Mahler tried to do too much. His excesses can be heard in the exhaustive tension in some of his music and in the repetitions. His symphonies are long, and they lack unity. They all begin to sound alike, and many times the composer finds it difficult to bring the music to a close. But having said that, there are many passages of overwhelming beauty.

Mahler the symphonist cannot be separated from Mahler the song composer. He was at his best when writing for the voice. For Mahler, music was a vision, intoxication, and fulfillment—"a mysterious language from beyond." His best-known work and masterpiece, which he never heard performed, is *Das Lied von der Erde (The Song of the Earth)*. It is a song cycle for solo voices and orchestra. Mahler seeks to describe a problem fundamental to all human beings—the reality of loneliness and death. In the music one hears the dualism of joy and despair, and one feels the fierce clinging to the beauty of earthly things, but mingled with resignation. It is a work that is solitary and unique, an expression of an artist upon whom darkness has fallen.

The haunting motif of the first movement is "Dark is Life, dark is death." The last movement may be regarded as Mahler's farewell to life. He wrote *The Song of the Earth* soon after his physician had told him he had a fatal heart ailment. It contains some of the saddest music ever written. The bitter poignancy of the contralto's last phrase "ewig" (everlasting), "ewig . . ." is unforgettable. Bruno Walter says that most people of his time were able to make some kind of peace between themselves and the universe. Mahler never could, just as fewer and fewer people can today. Mahler questioned the whole basis of his existence, never really finding an answer to the tormenting question, "For what?" But God has given us sufficient evidence in the Bible and in the Person of the Lord Jesus Christ and through the glory and wonder of His creation that our lives do have significance now and forever. No one has to go through life yearning for faith. Each person who places his or her hope in Christ can echo the truthful words of Paul: "For I know Whom I have believed and am persuaded that He is able to keep that which I have committed unto Him against that day" (2 Tim. 1:12).

Recommended Reading

Mahler, Alma. *Gustav Mahler: Memories and Letters*. New York: The Viking Press, 1946.

Redlich, H. F. *Bruckner and Mahler*. London: J. M. Dent and Sons, 1955.

Recommended Listening

Mahler: *Kindertotenlieder (Songs on the Death of Children)*
Des Knaben Wunderhorn (Youth's Magic Horn)

Das Lied von der Erde (The Song of the Earth)
Lieder eines Fahrenden Gesellen (Songs of a
Wayfarer)
9 Symphonies

Bruckner: Symphony No. 9
      Te Deum

Chapter XVI
Claude Achille Debussy
(1862—1918)

"A lost soul under a sky full of stars."—Thompson

"Everything he does is wrong," said one of his teachers, "but he is wrong in a talented way." Claude Debussy went to the Paris Conservatory and studied there for 11 contention-filled years, questioning and breaking away from all the rules of the past. "Why must dissonant chords always be resolved?" Debussy asked, and when he was not given a satisfactory answer he began to experiment with chromaticism, modal technique, the whole tone and pentatonic scales, the avoiding of a definite key, and using chords that tended to produce vagueness of tonality. With his fastidious ear he had a natural affinity for the exotic and old as well as the most avant-garde. He acquired a reputation as an iconoclast, violating all rules, and it is not surprising that some years later the 20th-century revolution in music began in France with Claude Debussy.

One of his professors at the Conservatory inquired, "What rules do you observe?" Debussy answered, "None, only my own pleasure!" "That's all very well," came the reply, "provided you're a genuis." They soon began to suspect he was.

One critic said of Debussy, "It is the beginning of the 20th-century breakup of music." In fact, everything in Western music has been called into question since 1910, and the two contemporary composers involved were Debussy and Schönberg, both rejecting what they considered "the strait jacket" of tonality. Oscar Thompson says that Debussy's music was the determining factor in the music of at least the first third of the 20th century. Other critics say that Debussy led straight to Webern.

Claude Debussy was born near Paris of a middle-class family. His father ran a not very successful china shop. It makes one think of the painter, Renoir, who worked in a china factory and was enchanted with color. A born rebel, Debussy attended no formal school, but because he played the piano well, he came to the attention of a wealthy lady who had been a pupil of Chopin. She taught him for three years without pay and so carefully that Debussy entered the Paris Conservatory in 1873 when he was 11 years old.

The years at the Conservatory were stormy because of his marked originality, and his youth was spent in unusual circumstances, even for talented musicians. Unexpectedly, at 18, while still living with his parents in a poor suburb of Paris and attending the Conservatory in the daytime, he came under the patronage of Madame Nadejda von Meck of Russia, the beloved friend of Tchaikovsky.

Madame von Meck, an extremely wealthy widow, engaged Debussy to play duets with her and her children. In the long summer vacations he traveled with the family to their palatial residences in Europe to teach the children music. Through Madame von Meck, Debussy's musical horizons suddenly widened. While they were in Venice, he met Wagner and immediately fell under the spell of *Tristan and Isolde.*

Debussy was with the von Mecks several summers. In Russia he was influenced by the music of Mussorgsky and Borodin. A remarkable sight reader, Debussy was especially entreated to play Tchaikovsky's music. Becoming accustomed to luxurious living as a youth had an unhealthy influence on Debussy. Later he delighted in confessing his fondness for every kind of indulgence. He had aristocratic tastes and especially liked caviar.

In Paris, around this time (he was 19), Debussy fell in love with a singer, Blanche Vasnier, the young wife of a well-known Parisian architect. She inspired many of his early compositions. When he was 22 Debussy won the Grand Prix de Rome, the highest award a young French composer can achieve. He received the prize because of his composition, a cantata, *The Prodigal Child.* He went to Rome intending to stay three years in the Villa Medici to pursue his creative work, but he hated being there. His only memorable experience in Rome was hearing Liszt play for the last time in his life at the Villa Medici. After two years Debussy returned to Paris. But before returning to France he made a long pilgrimage to Sant'Agata and chatted with Verdi as the beloved Italian composer planted vegetables with the assistance of a small boy. It was in Rome that he composed the orchestral piece, *Printemps* (Springtime), inspired by Botticelli's *Primavera*.

Debussy returned to Blanche and several other women. So that I will not have to repeat a number of unpleasant stories, it is enough to say that Debussy lived a life of extreme intemperance. One of his mistresses, "Gaby of the green eyes" (his favorite color), threatened suicide; his first wife Lily, a dressmaker, shot herself, though not fatally, and Debussy thought of killing himself too; but instead, he divorced Lily and married Emma Bardac, the mother of his illegitimate daughter. This last marriage seemed to succeed, although Debussy was never out of financial trouble because of his gourmet tastes. For his daughter Chouchou he later wrote the piano suite *The Children's Corner,* and the ballet for children, *The Toy Box.*

Debussy has been described by numerous epithets: unsociable, amorous, catlike, sensual, hedonistic, voluptuous, rebellious. He was supremely indifferent to the opinions of others. Debussy was not attractive looking. He had a large forehead which gave him an unbalanced appearance. He cared little for people, preferring cats to human beings. He had a sullen "I don't care" attitude toward life. Debussy thought only of himself and was incapable of making any sacrifice. A convinced atheist, he once said, "I have made a religion out of mysterious nature." Debussy was lazy about everything but his music.

On his return to Paris, he began to frequent salons where the avant-garde gathered. At Stephane Mallarmé's home he met some of the leading Impressionist and Symbolist painters. Debussy was a product of the movement called Symbolism, and he much preferred this term to Impressionism. A key to the Symbolists were the writings of Edgar Allan Poe. Baudelaire had translated and introduced Poe and his strange, horror-filled, hallucinated world to the French. The refined poetry of Verlaine, Baudelaire, and Mallarmé suggested to Debussy a new type of music—a music that seems to hint rather than to state. It is music which is vague, with tonal colors taking the place of logical development. Debussy thought of music as an expressive or suggestive medium. Romain Rolland called him "This great painter of dreams."

In the Exposition of 1889 Debussy heard some musicians from the Far East perform, and he was fascinated by the intricate percussive rhythms and bewitching instrumental colors which seemed to open a new world of sonority for him. Debussy felt closer to poets and painters than to other musicians. He especially liked Whistler. There was scarcely any Western music that he liked. He showed very little sympathy for or interest in what other musicians were creating.

In 1894, when he was 32, he completed his first major orchestral work, *Prelude to the Afternoon of a Faun*, and here his style was fully formed. In this tone poem inspired by Mallarmé a sensuous, enchanted world seems to rise before us, but far off and misty. It evokes the warmth of a summer day. With its color, mood, and harmonic opulence it is a late offshoot of Romanticism, actually a bridge between classical and 20th-century concepts of tonality. In this beautiful composition we are listening to one of the great inventors in the history of music. Though not loud music, in a sense it broke sound barriers because it was unlike any music of the past. It is fragmented, with shimmering vibrations, and the emphasis is on individual voices rather than the massive effects of Wagner. There are no superfluous notes in the scores of Debussy.

He had his years of being under the spell of Wagner. A fellow-composer, Erik Satie, urged Debussy to return to simplicity and clarity, expressing the French spirit in concise, luminous pieces, not to imitate the overblown Wagnerian forms. Satie was an early Dadaist, and his music is anti-Romantic. After Debussy freed himself from the Wagnerian influence, he fought Wagner the rest of his life. As Thompson shows, Debussy one said: "Wagner has led music astray into sterile and pernicious paths. Already for Beethoven the art of development consists in repetition, in the incessant restatement of identical themes; and Wagner has exaggerated this procedure to the point of caricature."

In 1900 the Three Nocturnes, *Nuages,* (Clouds) *Fêtes,* (Festivals) and *Sirènes* (Sirens), were performed with great success. The most obvious thing about these nocturnes is their relationship to Impressionist painting. It is as if the "sick room" of Romanticism had opened into a garden filled with flowers. Debussy· may have borrowed the names from Whistler. Specifically, *Nuages* has been likened to Monet, *Fêtes* to Renoir, and *Sirènes* to Turner.

As contrasting moods and evocations of light effects, these nocturnes are unique in music.

The turning point in Debussy's career came in 1902 with the première of his opera *Pelléas and Mélisande*, with words by Maeterlinck. It is the most important opera that Impressionism produced and is absolutely original, unlike any other opera. There is a flow of inner life in *Pelléas and Mélisande*, and Debussy forces us to listen less with our minds and more with our nerves. Debussy called it the "old and sad tale of the woods." The opera stirred up controversy because of its unconventional style and mysterious atmosphere. Debussy and the librettist declared that they were haunted in the work by the terrifying nightmare tale of Edgar Allan Poe's "The Fall of the House of Usher." For years Debussy worked on two operas, *The Devil in the Belfry* and *The Fall of the House of Usher* (both stories by Poe), but for various reasons neither was completed. In *The Devil in the Belfry* Debussy was going to have the devil whistle rather than sing.

With his second wife, Emma Bardac, who had divorced her banker husband, Debussy fled to Eastbourne, England, in 1905 to seek a refuge from the gossip and scandal they had stirred up in Paris. These troubles did not interfere with Debussy's creativity. The 15 years following *Pelléas and Mélisande* were productive ones for the composer.

La Mer (The Sea) written in 1905 is a masterpiece. This symphonic work presents three aspects of the sea—"The Sea from Dawn until Noon," "Sport of the Waves," and "Dialogue of the Wind and the Sea." It is a world of sheer fantasy. The sound is transparent and airy. It is the very essence of the sea, yet vague and mysterious. The orchestration is full of surprises and shattering climaxes—and Debussy exhibits rare strength and energy. *La Mer* reminds one of what Mallarmé said, "I think there should be nothing but illusion." Debussy never tells a story; he gives an impression. He had a passion for the sea. His father had wanted him to be a sailor, but Debussy wanted to be a painter. In *La Mer* we hear a "musical painting."

Some composers are imitative followers of others and lack a unique, distinctive style, but not Debussy. He is one of the most original of all composers. One quickly learns to recognize the works of this most intimate, personal musician.

Debussy wrote some exquisite songs, including "La Chevelure" (Tresses) in the set *Chansons de Bilitis* with words by his friend, Pierre Louÿs. Among the chamber works, Debussy's Quartet in G Minor is one of the greatest quartets written by a Frenchman.

In 1912 Debussy wrote *Images* for orchestra which includes "Iberia", one of the most famous interpretations of Spain. Debussy is concerned with sights, sounds, and a feeling for the Spanish dance. Here the objective universe has disintegrated into a world of dream and illusion, of mist and shadows. In the second movement, a tender night song called "Perfumes of the Night," we have veiled, languid sounds. This slow movement is one of Debussy's finest.

In his solo flute piece, *Syrinx* (Panpipes), also written in 1912, many features of Debussy's style occur in a short piece. Here there is sound for sound's sake rather than stress on content. It is full of wavering uncertainty, and intricate rhythms tend to free the music from the bar line. There is a sense of hesitation and vagueness. Debussy opened up new regions of sound and functionless harmony. He tends to write in patterns rather than with a sense of direction. There is fragmentation and a feeling of disintegration, yet the music is still beautiful.

The piano was Debussy's favorite instrument, and here he achieved his most sensitive speech. Three composers have been essential to piano music, Beethoven, Chopin, and Debussy. The aim of Debussy was to liberate the piano from its percussive sound. He said, "Beethoven definitely wrote badly for the piano." Debussy wanted the piano to sound like an instrument without hammers. Even though there is a nebulous quality in his piano pieces, Debussy had a superb command of compositional technique. He detested variations and obvious devices of formal development. He once said, "I think it is altogether disastrous to repeat oneself."

One of his best known pieces is "Claire de Lune" from the *Suite bergamasque*. His two glittering books of preludes for piano are pieces with a perfect sense of proportion for small things. "Reflections in the Water" (from *Images*) is a lovely piece written in excellent taste that reminds one of Monet, who lived in a houseboat so he could paint the water and light at different hours of the day. Someone has remarked that in Debussy's music there is always the sound and movement of water. One learns to love the cool pastel colors of Debussy. But there is a sadness because one hears in the compositions of Debussy and sees in Monet's paintings the adoring pantheist loving creation rather than the Creator.

Another famous water piece is Maurice Ravel's *Jeux d'Eau* (Fountains) with its use of the pentatonic scale. It was written before any of Debussy's important piano compositions and proves that Ravel was far less indebted to Debussy than some would claim.

Debussy acted as a musical critic for several periodicals to help out financially at times. Often he wrote under the pseudonym, M. Croche, and he was considered one of the wittiest critics of the century. His last years were less productive because of cancer, yet he always got back to music. It was there that he really lived his life. "I have no hobbies," he explained. "They never taught me anything but music." I am certain his professors at the Conservatory were impressed to hear that the unteachable Debussy learned something from their teaching.

In his last works he turned to the heritage of the French

Enlightenment composers Rameau and Couperin, and his style became more austere. His sonatas for cello and piano, and violin and piano, are almost Neo-classical. He became more depressed as his illness weakened him. In one of Debussy's last letters he wrote, "I am a poor traveler waiting for a train that will never come anymore." During the bombardment of Paris in March 1918 Debussy died. The funeral procession passed through deserted streets while his beloved city was being bombarded by enemy shells. His daughter, Chouchou, whom he loved dearly, died one year later at the age of 14.

Debussy adhered to no religion, although he was very superstitious. Lockspeiser says, "His atheism was sensual and instinctive. Quite simply he experienced no desire for a religion." He wrote no sacred music. Debussy once said, "We have not the simple faith of other days."

I personally deeply appreciate the music of Debussy—as does anyone who loves what is beautiful. But it makes me sad when I think of his life and the influence he has had on the musicians who have followed him. We must not forget the message of Debussy's music: humanism disintegrating into fragments and despair.

Recommended Reading

Lockspeiser, Edward. *Debussy*. New York: McGraw Hill, 1972.

Thompson, Oscar. *Debussy: Man and Artist*. New York: Tudor Publishing Co., 1940.

Recommended Listening

Chansons de Bilitis
Children's Corner Suite
Danses Sacrée et Profane
Ibéria
Images pour Piano (Books 1 and 2)

La Mer
Nocturnes
Pelléas et Mélisande
The Afternoon of a Faun
Preludes for Piano (Books 1 and 2)
Quartet in G Minor

Chapter XVII

Frederick Delius
(1862—1934)

"No matter what the motive, withdrawal from the world, if even for but a brief period, has usually been the first step that a man has taken on the road to high endeavour."— Eric Fenby

A blind cellist once said, "Only the music of Delius can convey to me some idea what it must be like to see a glowing sunset." As one of his friends said, "Delius was on the whole a watercolorist of music, not a filler of canvasses with oil."

Frederick Delius, who was to become one of the most poetic and artistic of composers, had an adventurous, often dissipated, troubled life. He was a sickly child, but he grew into a vigorous, lively, and handsome young man. He was one of 12 children.

Delius's father, a proud, unbending individual, was a successful German manufacturer who made a fortune in the wool business. He became a British subject in 1860 and settled in Bradford, England, where Delius was born. Even though his father appreciated music and invited musicians to perform in their home, he was indignant to think his son wanted to devote his life to what he regarded "a pleasant pastime" with little possibility of earning money. Sir Thomas Beecham, in an attempt to defend Delius's father and the hard stand he took against his son becoming a musician, says, "Neither he nor anyone else in his circle had the slightest idea that Frederick had in him a spark of original talent as a composer."

Delius's mother, also proud and unbending, gave him no encouragement, either. Even after their son had become a famous composer, his parents never forgave him for choosing to be a musician, and they refused ever to hear one note of his music.

Delius had no choice but to attend the International College to learn how to work in an office, and when he was 19 he entered the family business. He was not exactly an asset in the office and soon was transferred to Germany. There he spent the greater part of his time taking violin lessons, practicing, and going to concerts. In 1882 he was moved up to Sweden. At first he seemed to be doing well and orders came in to the Bradford office from the north. But then Delius discovered the beautiful Swedish countryside and the Norwegian mountains and fjords. . . . And so it went.

In 1884 after a violent family scene, Frederick at the age of 21 sailed for Florida where he was supposed to superintend an orange grove. Delius was fascinated by the music he heard while sitting on the porch of his cottage on warm summer nights near the bank of the St. Johns River. Anything natural and unspoiled appealed to him, and he was amazed at the exotic beauty around him. Years later he said, "Hearing the Negroes singing in such romantic surroundings; it was then and there that I first felt the urge to express myself in music."

One day when he was in Jacksonville, he went into a

music store and finding a piano in a back room sat down and began to improvise. Another visitor in the store was struck by the uncommon sounds coming from the back of the shop and introduced himself. Delius was delighted to meet another musician. His new friend was Thomas F. Ward, an organist and gifted teacher, who had come south for his health. Years later, Delius declared that the only teaching of any real value he ever received was from Ward. The organist must have enjoyed teaching him the next six months as Delius was enthusiastic and hungry for musical knowledge. Among many things, Ward taught Delius counterpoint, fugue, and good work habits. The one thing that saddened the teacher was his pupil's strong rejection of Christianity.

Within a year Delius had had enough of managing the orange grove—by now in a ruinous state—and when a brother came to see him he was glad to turn over the responsibility to him. After a short stay in Danville, Virginia, as a music teacher at the Roanoke Female College where he made his only appearance as a soloist in Mendelssohn's Violin Concerto, his father finally agreed to finance his musical study in Leipzig. His parents were amazed to learn that Frederick had been heralded as a celebrity in Danville and had also earned money teaching music, and they thought if he had a European diploma he could return to America and "do even better."

Delius felt he learned little in Leipzig, but there he met Edvard Grieg who was a tremendous help and encouragement to him in his musical understanding. Grieg, who became Delius's friend and believed he had talent, met the elder Delius on a trip to England. Even though the wool merchant was not convinced his son would amount to anything, Grieg interceded for the composer, and the father refrained from cutting off his allowance. Delius was not a good student but finally received his diploma because of the compositions he wrote.

After graduation he moved to Paris and lived there for over eight years with frequent long visits in Norway which inspired some of his most beautiful music. He had a generous uncle in Paris who also helped him financially. During one of his stays in Norway, he was aimlessly looking over the books in the library of a friend when he came across a copy of Nietzsche's *Thus Spake Zarathustra.* Even as a boy, Delius was at heart a pagan, and finding this book was one of the most important events in his life. As Eric Fenby says, "Nor did he rest content until he had read every work of Nietzsche that he could lay his hands on; and the poison entered into his soul."

In his Parisian period, Delius associated mainly with writers and painters. Two of his close friends were Strindberg, the playwright, and Edvard Munch, the painter—as one critic commented, "two super-egoists like himself." Another friend was Alfred Sisley, the impressionist painter. Both Delius and Sisley were of English origin and the sons of prosperous industrialists. Delius in a real sense may be thought of as the Sisley of music. They were both "painters" of water and light, and both men disliked excess in their artistic expression. Gauguin was also a friend of Delius. After Delius' uncle died and left him a legacy, he bought Gauguin's now-famous painting, *Nevermore* (he was later forced to sell it).

It was in Paris that Delius met his future wife, Jelka Rosen. Jelka was a gifted young painter with a Danish-Jewish background. She also loved music, poetry, and the philosophy of Nietzsche. He found her a stimulating companion, but that was all at the time.

The years Delius spent in Paris were strange. He had a period when he showed a decided preference for the "low life." Dressed in shabby clothes, he frequented all sorts of dubious quarters, the morgue included. He did work at his music on and off, hardly ever writing in the daytime, but he destroyed a considerable amount of it. Then for a while

he moved into the aristocratic "high life." Speedily he became a success, particularly among the women because he
was handsome and cosmopolitan. One of his talents which
won him friends was making horoscopes.

It is not surprising that he tired of this life, and one day
abruptly returned to Florida ostensibly "to attend to his
orange grove," but mainly it was to try and find a young
black woman to whom he had become attached many years
before. His search proved futile. He returned to France,
and shortly after turning up unannounced on Jelka's door-
step they were married.

In the meantime, Jelka and another artist, Ida Gerhardi,
with the help of Jelka's mother, had purchased a charming
old house in the village of Grez-sur-Loing on the southern
border of the Fontainebleau Forest. Close to the garden,
which is bordered by huge trees and slopes gently down to
the river, stands an old bridge which has been the subject
for many well-known paintings by such artists as Corot,
Sisley, Edvard Munch, and Carl Larsson. Larsson was fascinated with Grez. The studies he made there are those by
which he first won fame and now are in the National
Museum at Stockholm.

Grez-sur-Loing, which is about 40 miles from Paris, is
still a charming old village with narrow streets and houses
all wearing the color of antiquity. Not too long ago we had
the privilege of visiting Delius's two-storied home. The
present owner, Madame D'Aubigné, was very gracious.
She showed us Delius's music room, and even took time
to walk with us in the garden down to the Loing River
where Delius derived much inspiration for his music. The
composition *In a Summer Garden* captures the beauty and
tranquillity of this sun-drenched, riverside garden. It is
one of Delius's small masterpieces.

Delius lived over 35 years in Grez, from 1897 until his
death in 1934. After he settled in Grez he seldom heard or
thought about any music but his own. Delius, the poet

always, was able to recollect emotion in tranquillity. Here he lived a very sheltered existence that revolved wholly around his work. Jelka was the ideal wife for Delius. As Fenby observed, "Her name deserves a very prominent place on the scroll of those who have given themselves unstintingly for others." Had Delius not married Jelka, we might never have heard of him, because he was not a man who knew how to organize his life. Jelka did it for him, because she believed in his genius and she loved him.

It was never easy to be in the company of Delius, even in the early years at Grez, because of his aloofness, his indifference to whether he hurt the feelings of people or not, his colossal egotism, his contempt for "ordinary" village people, his unbearable selfishness, and his inability to be interested in anything other than his music. He did enjoy a good table, and there was always a well-stocked wine cellar in the Delius home.

It took many years, but finally Delius's works aroused interest in Germany and later in England. Sir Thomas Beecham, who was responsible for introducing the music of Delius to the English people and who was a great interpreter of his works, was amazed when he first met Delius because he looked so unlike an artist. "He must be a cardinal," thought Beecham upon the first meeting. Delius did have an air of sober elegance, shrewdness, and fastidiousness one associates with high-ranking ecclesiastics.

His life became more difficult and his appearance even more austere as he approached the age of 60. He fell victim to blindness and creeping paralysis because of syphilis which he had contracted as a young man, and the last 12 years of his life were spent as an invalid. After he lost the use of his hands, he resumed composing when an unusual young man came to be his amanuensis. Eric Fenby has written a very readable book about his experiences in Grez entitled *Delius as I Knew Him.*

Delius the man (like Wagner) is difficult to like, but not

his music. Those who respond to the magic of his sound find it some of the most beautiful ever written. He was a composer of instinct, rather than intellect. His was a "still, small voice," but an absolutely unique one. The music of Delius is suffused with rapture. It is fluid, like light and water. He was a sensitive nature poet and his music has the emotional quality we associate with British poetry. Delius was a watercolorist using notes instead of paint. Because he was an ardent lover of that which is beautiful in nature, we not only hear his music, but it is as if we are seeing impressionistic paintings of hills, trees, birds, sunrises, and sunsets.

Many critics think the compositions of Delius are suggestive of England, but Eric Fenby felt that the mellow French countryside near Grez-sur-Loing and Delius's own garden, as well as what he had heard and seen in Florida and Norway in his earlier years were the true source of his inspiration. In speaking about composition, Delius said, "You can't teach a young musician to compose any more than you can teach a delicate plant how to grow, but you can guide him a little by putting a stick in there. . . . How can music ever be a mere intellectual speculation or a series of curious combinations of sound that can be classified like the articles in a grocer's shop? Music is an outburst of the soul."

The development of Delius as a composer was unusually slow. At the age of 41 he had written five operas, six large works for orchestra, several suites, a number of short pieces, and about 50 songs, and of this output only a few of the songs had been published.

One of his earliest compositions was *Over the Hills and Far Away*. Delius, having rejected the God of history, found his inspiration in nature. His early works have a certain vigor and freshness, but as he grew older his attempts at gaiety have an air of sadness. His later efforts have an increasing atmosphere of despair and melancholy which has a deep effect on the sensitive listener.

He dedicated his orchestral suite *Florida* to the people of Florida. He first arranged to have it performed when he was a student in Leipzig and paid the members of the orchestra by treating them to a barrel of beer.

Delius's Piano Concerto shows the influence of Grieg. Delius tended to begin his works softly, but not in this composition. The one-movement concerto has a forte opening. It is strong, rhapsodic music. There are moments in the music of Delius that are meandering and dull, and one is often aware of his lack of formal training. The best of music is more than "an outburst of the soul."

In 1902 he wrote *Appalachia.* It refers to North America and especially the Mississippi River. The Civil War had ended only 19 years before Delius went to Florida, and he saw some of the tragedy of the reconstruction era. In *Appalachia* Delius uses variations on an old slave song, "No Trouble in that Land Where I'm Bound." The second tune he uses is, "Oh, Honey, I'm Goin' Down the River in the Morning." It is a song of separation and heartbreak. "Goin' down the river" meant to be sold and separated from one's family.

In *Sea Drift* (1904) Delius uses a text from Walt Whitman's *Leaves of Grass.* It is a setting of the middle section of the poem, "Out of the Cradle Endlessly Rocking." The music evokes the surge of the sea which symbolizes the intensity of love and longing which is the composer's real theme. The story is of two birds and their nest of eggs hidden in a briar close to the seashore. The she-bird disappears. The he-bird, watching the nest, continues looking out at the sea, waiting in vain for her return.

His most outstanding opera is *A Village Romeo and Juliet.* The orchestral interlude, "A Walk to the Paradise Garden," is exquisite. One notices the Wagnerian influence of the *Tristan and Isolde* chord at the end.

One of Delius's compositions, *A Song Before Sunrise,* captures in a sweeping cadence the exhilaration and freshness of an early morning in the Swiss Alps.

Brigg Fair (1907) is one of Delius's most widely performed works. It is an English Rhapsody in the form of variations on a popular tune. It was first performed in Basel, Switzerland. Some of the critics say that after *Brigg Fair* Delius only repeated himself. It may be true, but he bears repetition.

One of the most exquisite pieces ever written about the Springtime is his composition, *On Hearing the First Cuckoo in Spring.* It is for a small orchestra and probably was inspired by the beautiful countryside of Norway, which Delius loved. As Sir Thomas Beecham says, "There is a world of sorrow in one little song."

Before mentioning the composition *A Mass of Life,* with words from Nietzsche's *Thus Spake Zarathustra,* it would be helpful to give some background information about the German philosopher, Friedrich Nietzsche. His father was a Lutheran minister, and behind each of his parents was a line of clergymen. Nietzsche's father died when he was five and the delicate, brilliant child was raised in a household of adoring women who did not equip the boy for the shocks of the real world outside. At the university he quickly succumbed to the philosophy of Schopenhauer, and within a few years Nietzsche had developed the doctrine of the Superman. But because he, like Schopenhauer, worked out his philosophy without a true base and reference point, after some years he learned that his new values did not satisfy him. He became more and more cynical. He thought of himself as a nihilist, but he found out that it is nearly impossible to live wholly negatively. He suffered dreadfully in his life. He had syphilis, became a drug addict, and at the age of 45 he lost his reason. The tragedy is that already he had put into print the ideas he no longer believed in, but Delius wholeheartedly adopted Nietzsche's philosophy as his gospel, and *A Mass of Life* not only gives insight into Nietzsche's thinking but also Delius's. It is loud, unattractive music. Delius often does not write well for the voice. But as in much of Delius, there are the moments of beauty. Some consider it the climax of his achievement, although it is less often performed than his smaller orchestral pieces.

A Mass of Life is an attack upon Christian doctrine and the Christian way of life as Nietzsche and Delius saw it. They both wanted to correct what they called the "slave morality" of Christianity. Their great emphasis was upon will, not bowing to anyone, and living and dying fearlessly though death be total extinction.

Death when it came to Delius was terrible, and within a few months his steadfast wife was dead too.

In speaking about Delius, Eric Fenby observes, "Given those great natural musical gifts and that nature of his, so full of feeling, and which at its finest inclined to that exalted end of man which is contemplation, there is no knowing to what sublime heights he would have risen had he chosen to look upwards to God instead of downwards to man!"

When we drive over the St. Bernard pass to Italy, often we listen to the music of Delius which heightens the beauty of the world we see around us, but then we are glad to turn to Bach and Handel who fill our hearts with wonder, not only at all the marvel and mystery of our world, but at the God of all creation. When one believes the Scriptures, there is a true reason for hope and rejoicing. Christians are not victims of a "slave morality." They bow down willingly before the everlasting God, "Who at sundry times and in diverse manners spoke in time past unto the fathers by the prophets, [and] hath in these last days spoken unto us by his Son, whom he hath appointed heir of all things, by whom also he made the worlds" (Hebrews 1:1 and 2).

Recommended Reading

Beecham, Sir Thomas. *Frederick Delius.* London: Hutchinson, 1960.

Fenby, Eric. *Delius as I Knew Him.* London: Icon Books, 1966.

Jefferson, Alan. *Delius.* London: J. M. Dent, 1972.

Recommended Listening

Appalachia
Brigg Fair
Concerto in C Minor for Piano
In a Summer Garden
On Hearing the First Cuckoo in Spring
Over the Hills and Far Away
Sea Drift
Song Before Sunrise
Summer Evening
Walk to the Paradise Garden
Florida Suite

Chapter XVIII
Arnold Schönberg
(1874—1951)

"If it is art it is not for all, and if it is for all it is not art."—Schönberg

The only instruction in composition Arnold Schönberg*
had was studying counterpoint for a few months with a
musician friend, Alexander von Zemlinsky (1872-1942).
Yet today Schönberg is known as the most controversial
and cerebral composer in history. Rosenfeld called him
"the great troubling presence in modern music."

In reply Schönberg said, "I personally hate to be called a
revolutionist, which I am not. What I did was neither revolutionary nor anarchy." His followers are completely in
accord with him. They feel Schönberg carried to a logical
conclusion the culmination of the 1,000-year-old tradition
of European polyphony. But there are other outstanding

---

*Arnold Schonberg prefered to spell his name Schoenberg later
in life, but since most works list it as Schönberg, the publishers
thought it best to use that spelling.

musicians who feel differently. The famous Swiss conductor, Ansermet, in speaking of the breakdown in communication between composer and audience, said that perhaps the new music was so alien to the normal processes of thought and aural experience that it was based on a faulty aesthetic.

Arnold Schönberg was born in Vienna. Both his parents enjoyed music. By the age of eight he began to study the violin and soon after made his first attempt at composing. When his father died suddenly, the young Schönberg had already left school in order to devote his life to music. Because of this unexpected tragedy, he grew up in straightened circumstances. Nearly all his life he struggled financially. He went to work in a bank to earn a living and composed in off-hours. Schönberg studied and worked entirely alone, and basically was a self-taught composer. But as is the custom in Vienna, he used to meet daily with Zemlinsky and other musicians in a café for exchanging ideas. Through Zemlinsky he was introduced to the advanced musical circles in Vienna which at the turn of the century were under the spell of *Tristan* and *Parsifal*. All of this was part of Schönberg's learning experience.

Basically a philosopher, Schönberg had a strong taste for abstract speculation and the German reverence for "the idea." He had long periods of not composing while thinking through and developing his theories. There is no doubt that Arnold Schönberg had one of the most original minds of all time and that his influence has been overwhelming.

Like many Austrian-Jewish intellectuals of his generation he became a Roman Catholic. Then for a while he turned toward Protestantism. But in 1933 when Hitler came to power and Schönberg was forced to leave Europe, he found it spiritually necessary to return to the Hebrew faith. Schönberg was a seeker after truth until he died, but it is not clear what he meant by the word "truth." He said once, "My religion needs no God, only faith."

In 1899 Schönberg composed in three weeks the sextet *Verklärte Nacht* (Transfigured Night). Everything that he wrote was composed in an incredibly short time because it was already worked out in his mind. The piece met with outrage, and when the audience hissed the performers, they sat down calmly and played it again. The composition uses the chromatic idiom of Wagner's *Tristan*. There are restless modulations, wandering sounds, and a building up of tension. It is written in the Expressionistic style reminiscent of the paintings of Munch, Kirchner, and Kokoschka. The music has exaggerated wide leaps and extreme ranges to portray hyper-emotion. Today it is one of Schönberg's most popular works.

After his marriage to Zemlinsky's sister, Mathilde, the couple moved to Berlin in 1901. In order to earn their living, the serious, intellectual Schönberg accepted a position conducting operettas and music-hall songs. It is hard to believe, but he even wrote a cabaret song; however, it was never performed because it was too difficult.

Soon they were back in Vienna, and they moved in with Zemlinsky. Because he was a gifted teacher, Schönberg gathered about him a band of disciples. The two key pupils who helped to advance his ideas creatively were Alban Berg and Anton Webern. Most of his students worshiped him, and they helped to sustain Schönberg in the fierce battle for recognition that was ahead of him. The group became known as the "Second Viennese School." In his textbook, *Theory of Harmony,* he said at the beginning, "This book I have learned from my pupils." In 1900 some of Schönberg's songs were performed, "and ever since that day," he once remarked, "the scandal has never ceased." It is curious that Schönberg in his theory classes rarely taught his own music, but basically concentrated on the compositions of Bach, Mozart, Haydn, Schubert and Brahms.

In 1903 he became acquainted with Mahler who was one of his strongest supporters and promoters. When the

Chamber Symphony Opus 9 by Schönberg was presented a few years later, the audience whistled and banged their seats to protest "such sounds," but Mahler sprang up in his box and commanded silence. Afterwards Mahler confided to his wife, Alma, "I do not understand his work. But then he is young and may well be right."

Schönberg's move away from tonality can be observed in the Second String Quartet (1907-1908). In the last movement there is a vocal part for soprano which opens with the words, "I feel air from another planet." This often has been symbolically interpreted in the light of Schönberg's breakthrough to a new world of sound.

In 1909 he finished his Piano Piece Opus II No. 1 which was the first composition ever to dispense completely with tonal means of organization and move towards atonality. The whole course of Post-romantic music exhibited a tendency toward atonality. Schönberg never liked the word "atonal." He preferred the word "pantonal," but atonal is what has taken root, because it sums up for most people what Schönberg's music expresses—the rejection of tonality.

In Western music tonality is based on the principle that seven of the 12 tones belong to a key, while five lie outside it. Schönberg took his departure from the last quartets of Beethoven, but the more powerful influence in Schönberg's desire to emancipate the dissonance and to have greater freedom was Wagner. In *Tristan* Wagner had pushed chromaticism as far as possible while still remaining within the boundaries of the key. Schönberg said that the time had come to do away with the distinction between the seven diatonic tones and the five chromatic ones, and so he took the next step and declared that the 12 tones must be treated as equals. In this decision Schönberg did more to change the sound of music in the 20th century than any other composer.

Hindemith, who was rooted in the Reformation and influenced by Schütz, Bach, and Händel, insisted that doing away with the tonic is like trying to do away with gravity in the physical world and results in chaos. He regarded the principle of tonality as an immutable law. Hindemith believed that order in a composition is symbolical of a higher order within the moral and spiritual universe, a doctrine taught by Augustine. As Machlis says, "Dissonance resolving to consonance is symbolically an optimistic act, affirming the triumph of rest over tension, of order over chaos."*

Schönberg was greatly influenced by the Expressionist painters Wassily Kandinsky, Paul Klee, and Franc Marc, as well as the poets Stefan George and Richard Dehmel. Expressionism sought to describe the inner state of man in the 20th century.

For a time Schönberg studied with Kandinsky, and between 1907 and 1910 Schönberg painted a large number of paintings. The hallucinatory visions of the Expressionist painters brought forth distorted images on the canvases, and in like manner, musical Expressionism rejected what had hitherto been accepted as beautiful. Expressionism was "the last gesture of a dying Romanticism." It was a suppressed, violent, agonized, distorted Romanticism of an anti-Romantic time in history, and the music of the age turned to atonality to try to express in notes what the artists were putting on canvas. Schönberg once said, "There is only one greatest goal towards which the artist strives: to express himself."

Also in 1909 Schönberg wrote his atonal monodrama, *Erwartung* (Expectation). It is an eerie story of a woman who wanders through the woods by night seeking her unfaithful lover. When she finds him, he is dead. Schönberg wanted to portray how, in moments of fearful tension, one

---

*J. Machlis, *Introduction to Contemporary Music* (New York: W. W. Norton and Company, 1961) p. 338

relives the whole of one's life. The work has a single character and requires a huge orchestra. Schönberg explored the world of fear and dreams. In his music, agony of soul often reigns unrelieved.

In 1912 he wrote *Pierrot lunaire* (Moonstruck Pierrot). One feels as if the music is suspended, because in order to avoid tonal centers and a place of return and rest, Schönberg used illogical root movements and no resolution. *Pierrot lunaire* is like surrealist poetry. Some feel it is his most significant score. The tone poem is a parallel to T. S. Eliot's *The Waste Land* which is a series of fragmentary dramatic monologues about the decadence of modern man.

The contralto part is not to be sung, but the rhythm must be kept while the voice only suggests pitches and immediately moves away from them. (This is called "speech-song.") It is extremely difficult to perform. Any means of exaggeration is used in order to communicate extreme human emotions. Schönberg was searching for some other way than the text to give unity in the composition, as if he was writing music for words that had no meaning for him. One is reminded of Munch's painting, *The Scream*. Schönberg, like the Dutch painter, Mondrian, rejected the laws of nature, and then had to set up his own laws, which instead of giving more freedom are more demanding and restricting.

In 1913 Schönberg completed *Die Glückliche Hand* (The Lucky Hand) with libretto by himself. In one scene the composer-painter uses both sound and color. A crescendo goes from red through brown, green and blue-gray to purple, red, orange, yellow, and finally white.

In the same year Schönberg had his first triumph with the performance of *Gurre-Lieder* in Vienna. It is considered the "grand finale" of the whole Wagnerian, Postromantic era. Schönberg remembering the hostility the public had shown toward his earlier works, when called to the stage again and again, bowed to the conductor, bowed to the orchestra, but in no way acknowledged the audience. "For years those people who greeted me with cheers tonight refused to recognize me," he said. "Why should I thank them for appreciating me now." Schönberg had a love-hate relationship with Vienna as Mahler did before him.

Another key work is the great unfinished oratorio, *Jacob's Ladder* (1917), based on the idea of reincarnation. In the text Schönberg said, "One must go on without asking what lies before or behind."

For seven years Schönberg did not write music while clarifying his thinking of how to reject tonality and still have unity rather than chaos, and thus the "12-tone" method was invented. The emphasis of the 12-tone method or serial writing, as it is also called, is intellectual and abstract. It is a rigidly organized system and moves within an extremely narrow expressive range. A *row* consists of the 12 tones of the octave in any order the composer decides. All 12 notes must be heard before any one recurs. This is to avoid a sense of return and resolution, or having one note sound more important than the others. All 12 notes are of the same importance. As Grout says, "Stated baldly, the theory *may sound* like a recipe for turning out music by machine." But he explains that it is not so. If the technique has been mastered, the 12-tone row no more inhibits a composer's spontaneity than do the rules for writing a tonal fugue.

The 12-tone row or serial technique represents Schönberg's concept of "perpetual variation" (a fragmented contrapuntal music without a base). It is used to project moods of anxiety and fear. "It is significant that the perpetual variation of the basic row functions somewhat like the ragas of Hindu music," says Grout.

In 1918 Schönberg founded the Society for Private Musical Performances with the intention of giving artists and art-lovers a real knowledge of modern music. Not only was the music of Schönberg performed, but also that of Berg, Webern, Bartok, Mahler, Debussy, etc. In the final concert in 1921 *Pierrot lunaire* was given.

In 1923 Schönberg's long silence was broken, and in the Five Piano Pieces of Opus 23, in the last of the set, the new 12-tone row technique was revealed. The same year Schönberg's wife died. The following summer he married Gertrude Kolisch, and in 1925 he was appointed professor of composition at the Berlin Academy of Arts. Here there was a favorable attitude toward experimental art, but with Hitler coming to power in 1933 Schönberg had to leave Germany. He went to the United States and eventually joined the faculty at the University of California in Los Angeles, where he continued to teach and compose. He wrote in 1947 A *Survivor from Warsaw* expressing grief over the victims of anti-Semitic persecution.

His American period in which he wrote a mixture of 12-tone and diatonic compositions was not as productive as the years before because of ill health. He was unable to finish his opera, *Moses and Aaron.* He completed two acts before he died. He wrote the libretto himself, and it is considered a masterpiece. It is based on the conflict that Moses is unable to communicate his vision and Aaron can communicate but does not really understand. In Schönberg's story Moses speaks of the "unknowable, impersonal God" which is the opposite of the truth. The Bible emphasizes the personal God whom anyone can know through Jesus Christ.

Schönberg said, "I believe that art comes not of ability but of necessity." He became a composer in spite of all that was against him. He was very disciplined, not only in his life, but in his music. Every trace of frivolity is missing. He was always burdened by serious, philosophic thoughts and labored over his compositions as if they were mathematical problems.

He grew increasingly rebellious and iconoclastic with

each succeeding work and continued to penetrate deeper into the world of musical abstraction. Schönberg aimed to strip music of human emotion, feeling, and relationships and wanted to produce music that was brief, thoroughly objective, and unemotional.

At times his egomania approached that of Wagner. Schönberg said of himself, "I have discovered something which will guarantee the supremacy of German music for the next 100 years." On another occasion he said, "Genius learns only from itself; talent chiefly from others." He seemed to take a grim pleasure in being the "troubling presence" of modern music. After he completed his Violin Concerto in 1936, he commented, "I am delighted to add another unplayable work to the repertoire."

Toward the end of his life, Schönberg was a bitter man, and resentful that he was neglected. Because of his inner torment, he begame increasingly distrustful and irritable. Pablo Casals visited Arnold Schönberg a few months before his death, and he found the composer sad and depressed because he thought he had done harm to music.

Schönberg, in speaking about what he believed, said, "There are comparatively few points on which I strictly adhere to the Bible." Yet interestingly enough, the last completed composition of Schönberg was Psalm 130, *Out of the Depths I Cry to Thee.* (De Profundis, Opus 50b) It is a 12-tone work for unaccompanied choir. According to Struckenschmidt, in it we hear "the daemonic compulsion that governed his music."

The teaching of Schönberg, with his "uncompromising style and extraordinary originality," profoundly influenced two of his pupils, Alban Berg (1885-1935) and Anton Webern (1883-1945). Berg adopted most of Schönberg's methods of construction, but used them with more freedom that allowed for progressions in harmony and tonal-sounding chords. Berg, the Expressionist, was drawn to librettos of violence and unusual behavior. In his opera

Wozzeck, which is a classic of the "Second Viennese
School," he turned to the unconscious and irrational in his
flight from reality, using themes of existential menace and
death. *Lulu* is a more complex, abstract opera based on the
12-tone row. Lulu is the eternal type of *femme fatale* "who
destroys everyone because she is destroyed by everyone."
It is a story of murder, blackmail and sexual perversion, to
the final degradation of the aging heroine on the streets of
London. When Berg composed, he locked himself in a
darkened room with the windows closed even in summer.
His was essentially a tragic, morbid, pessimistic view of life
which accorded with the intellectual climate in the twenties. He fought against chronic ill health and died at 50 of
blood poisoning.

Anton Webern wrote lonely, strange music which was
almost never performed in his lifetime. As a young man he
admired Wagner, then studied with Schönberg and followed the road of atonality. He grew increasingly partial to
fragmentary themes and broad leaps. These fragments are
pieced together into a mosaic consisting merely of brief,
seemingly unrelated sounds. Webern built upon the
Schönbergian doctrine of perpetual variation. Sometimes a
single tone became Webern's entire theme. It is sound for
sound's sake with a sense of hovering suspension. This
"pointillist" manner has had a vast influence, especially on
his disciples, Boulez and Stockhausen, as well as his concept of total serialization which means complete control of
the sonorous material. In Webern's Five Orchestral Pieces,
the longest composition lasts a minute, and the shortest 19
seconds. Webern wanted extreme brevity. It is music that
hovers on the brink of silence.

John Cage studied for awhile with Schönberg in California, but he turned from the iron-clad 12-tone system to the
opposite extreme of "chance" music.

In conclusion, it is to be observed that the 12-tone row
is limited as to the broad spectrum of human emotions it

can express. True, it effectively reflects the atmosphere of fear, despair, and hopelessness which is prevalent in our moment in history. It is the right background music for the many threatening and horror-filled films being shown today. Twelve-tone compositions often end with a question leaving the listener "up in the air," describing vividly modern man's sense of non-resolution. As Francis Schaeffer said in *How Should We Then Live?*, "This stands in sharp contrast to Bach who, on his biblical base, had much diversity but always resolution. Bach's music had resolution because as a Christian he believed that there will be resolution both for each individual and for history."

Milton Babbitt (1916—), a mathematician and composer of 12-tone music says, "I believe in cerebral music." He explains that one should no more expect the layman to understand present-day music than one would expect him to understand advanced physics or mathematics. I began this chapter with a quotation from Schönberg, "If it is art it is not for all, and if it is for all it is not art."

It is not surprising that Arnold Schönberg felt at the end of his life that he had done harm to music. A musical system which appeals only to an elitist group of scientists and abstract philosophers must be based on a faulty aesthetic, as Ansermet suggested. The 12-tone music and all the variations that have followed, have no joy, no humor, no optimism, and no sense of delight in God's world.

Every great artist has a world view, and certainly Schönberg is a key composer in music history. "We have arrived," says Paul Henry Lang, "at the age of the philosophical composer in the sense that he is not content, as a creator, with musical expression but feels compelled to present his music as an illustration of philosophical ideas." As art historian Hans Rookmaaker said in a recent lecture: "What started in the philosopher's study is now in the hearts and minds of the whole Western world." The philosophical music of Schönberg is a vivid illustration of this.

His influence has spread widely. Then it opened the door to electronic music which eliminated the performer, and today we have a "machine listening to a machine."

Schönberg loved Bach's music, but tragically he did not understand the spiritual content of his life and music. In place of the freedom, joy, and musical vitality of Bach, "Schönberg took the body of music and stripped it of flesh, muscle, heart, and pulse leaving it just a skeleton" (Stuckenschmidt).

I am not saying that the 12-tone row should not be used. It does express some aspects of life extremely well, but it is a limited system with a negative outlook. The prophet Jeremiah was also confronted with disaster and human despair throughout his life, but because of his faith in the infinite, personal God was able to say, "Of this I remind myself, therefore I still have hope: Because of the Lord's mercies we are not consumed; His compassions never fail. They are new every morning; great is Thy faithfulness" (Lamentations 3:21-23, Berkeley).

Recommended Reading

Reich, Willi. *Schoenberg: A Critical Biography*. New York: Praeger Publishers, 1971.

Stuckenschmidt, H. H. *Arnold Schoenberg*. London: John Calder, 1959.

Recommended Listening

Schönberg: Chamber Symphony in E, Opus 9
De Profundis Opus 506
Erwartung
Five Piano Pieces Opus 23
Gurre-Lieder
Moses and Aaron
Pierrot Lunaire

Variations for Orchestra Opus 31
Verklärte Nacht

Berg: *Wozzeck*

Webern: Five Orchestral Pieces Opus 10

Chapter XIX

Igor Stravinsky
(1882—1971)

"For a beginner, in whatever field, there is only one possiblity, namely to submit himself to an external discipline, with the double aim of learning the language of his profession, and, in the process, of forming his own personality."—Stravinsky

A friend (and Stravinsky had many friends) said that he looked like "a deeply preoccupied grasshopper." He was small of stature, five feet, four inches, and to change the metaphor, he was a dapper, birdlike, lively, little man. Stravinsky was close to ninety when he died. He lived long enough to be recognized as the world's greatest living composer. Harold Schonberg of the *New York Times* felt that Stravinsky had the strongest influence on the early part of the 20th century, Arnold Schönberg and his pupils on the latter part. Stravinsky was the least hide-bound and dogmatic, and most accessible of the great 20th-century composers.

Igor Stravinsky was born near St. Petersburg (now

Leningrad) in 1882. Since his father was a famous operatic bass, Stravinsky grew up in a musical atmosphere. The home was a center of culture, as the parents not only loved music, but books and art also. He began piano lessons at nine. Stravinsky said that as a child he was very lonely and reserved, partly because it was difficult for him to reveal his feelings. When he was still a boy his mother took him to the opera. There he saw and heard Glinka's *A Life for the Tsar.* He had already played through some of the music on the piano, and that performance was an unforgettable experience for the future composer. Even though music was a part of his life, his parents wanted him to study law, which he did.

At the University he became a friend of Rimsky-Korsakov's youngest son. It did not happen at once, but after Stravinsky proved himself to be a diligent student of music, he began his three years' study of composition with Rimsky-Korsakov. After a year and a half under such excellent teaching (Stravinsky became one of the great orchestrators), he began his first symphony.

About the same time he graduated in law from the University he married his cousin, Catherine Nossenko. As it was the custom in the Stravinsky family to go to the country in the summertime, Stravinsky promised Rimsky-Korsakov that he was going to send him a composition. By this time a strong bond of friendship had developed between the teacher and pupil. Stravinsky worked hard on his composition, *Fireworks,* and within six weeks it was mailed. In a few days the parcel returned with a message written on it: "Not delivered, owing to the death of the addressee."

Before his death, Rimsky-Korsakov arranged for some of Stravinsky's music to be performed. In the audience was Sergei Diaghilev, Director of the famous Russian Ballet Company, who had a genius for spotting talent. Diaghilev was a strong personality, and he inspired, stimulated, and dominated the music and art world between 1909 and 1929, calling on such talents as Debussy, Ravel, Matisse, Picasso, Cocteau, Satie, Poulenc, to mention a few.

Upon a single hearing of the *Fireworks,* Diaghilev commissioned Stravinsky to write an original ballet. Stravinsky chose a theme from an old Russian legend, and *The Firebird* was first performed in Paris in 1910. Overnight Stravinsky became famous. *The Firebird* was the first real modern ballet. This was followed in 1911 by *Petrouchka* which was a revolt against the sweet sound of Romanticism. Then in 1913 came *The Rite of Spring.* The première, as Onnen describes it, "led to a very memorable scandal of the type which Paris possesses an unquestionable monopoly."

When we listen to *The Rite of Spring* today we cannot grasp how shocking the ballet was to the Parisians because our ears have heard such an unbelievable array of sounds and noise since 1913. We have become unshockable listeners.

Stravinsky felt the scandal was the fault of Nijinsky, the choreographer—there were some rather indecent scenes—but the music was extremely *new,* and in itself had a startling effect on the listeners who had come for the usual romantic sounds and sights. *The Rite of Spring* occasioned an earthquake in the musical world. It was to the first half of the 20th century what Beethoven's Ninth Symphony and Wagner's *Tristan* were to the 19th century. It had a profound influence on other composers with its shattering rhythmical force. It is a masterpiece of controlled violence requiring a large orchestra. Stravinsky said that Debussy had the greatest influence on his writing *The Rite of Spring.*

About one year after the explosive evening, *The Rite of Spring* was performed as a concert number with tremendous success. The new rhythm of the *Rite* was as important as the rhythm of jazz, because something like it appears in most of Stravinsky's later compositions and in the music of a majority of composers after 1914. In a sense, Stravinsky has restored to music a healthy, unwavering pulse. Many of his compositions are suitable for dancing. His music makes a clean sound. He is never sentimental. His is a coldly intellectual art. Stravinsky said that the purpose of music is "to create order between things, and above all, an order between man and time." Stravinsky's music could be thought of as "thinking in sound." He said that the musicians of "my generation and I, myself, owe the most to Debussy."

Stravinsky continued to work in close collaboration with Diaghilev, but during World War I the Stravinskys lived mostly in Switzerland. He particularly enjoyed being in Clarens on Lake Geneva as it had meant so much to Tchaikovsky.

In 1917 the Russian Revolution shook the world. In addition to Stravinsky's understandable concern for relatives and friends, it caused him to be cut off from an important part of his financial resources. He took a strong stand against the Communist regime and did not return to his country for years. Soon after hearing of the revolution Stravinsky was confined to bed because of a nervous affliction. Years later he wrote about those days: "I found myself, with nothing in my pocket in a strange land, in the middle of a war, and so, whatever happened, I had to provide a means of existence for myself and my family. The only consolation I had," he added laconically, "was that my friends, Ansermet and Ramuz, were hardly in a stronger financial position than I."

The three friends, pooling their various abilities, went to work. The Swiss writer, Ramuz, wrote a libretto adapted from a Russian story, Stravinsky composed the music, and Ansermet was the director of L'Histoire du Soldat (The Soldier's Tale). It is a story of a soldier who barters his violin (the symbol of his soul) for the allurements of the devil. It was a very economical production, using few instruments and showing the influence of jazz. All they lacked was financial backing, and happily Werner Reinhart, the famous theatrical director was staying in Winterthur. They contacted him and interested him in their project. Soon they had the money. At the time *L'Histoire du Soldat* was not one of the most successful of Stravinsky's works, but today it is widely performed. To help himself get back on his feet again Stravinsky wrote various piano works and began appearing as a concert pianist and conductor. He always loved the piano.

As soon as World War I was over, Stravinsky moved to France and lived in various places there for about 20 years. In Paris he was in contact with artistic circles, including Erik Satie and "Les Six." Stravinsky moved and traveled a great deal, and wherever he went he was composing. In his French Period he abandoned the Russian features of his earlier style and adopted a Neo-classical idiom. It was a tremendous effort to change. One can see in studying Stravinsky's music that nearly every major work is preceded by a minor composition for a smaller orchestra.

In his Neo-classical period Stravinsky was drawn to the clear forms of the Baroque and Classic styles. He treated them in his ultra-modern fashion. He felt that music should not attempt to carry a message or mean anything in itself.

His work is that of one of the supreme logicians in composition. The music of Stravinsky is not meant to please an audience, nor arouse its passions, and because of this, his music has a lean sound. Personally, I prefer a rounder sound, but I admire him because of his concern for discipline, clarity, and tradition. He deplored the refusal of many artists to submit to the discipline of an established order. I believe that Stravinsky's music, as a whole, commands more respect than love.

He wrote another ballet for Diaghilev, *Pulcinella,* in

1920. In it Stravinsky plunged straight into the refreshing stream of the 18th-century Italian tradition. *Apollo* (1928) was the last of Stravinsky's ballets to be produced by the Russian Ballet Company. In 1929 Diaghilev died and the ballet company melted away.

In 1930 Stravinsky wrote his *Symphony of Psalms* dedicated to the glory of God. Grout says that it is one of the great works of the 20th century, a masterpiece of invention, musical architecture, and religious devotion. It is exceedingly terse and compact, lasting no more than 20 minutes. Here is Stravinsky at his best, inspired by a sincere religious conviction. Robert Craft, in his book *Conversations with Igor Stravinsky,* tells of the incident when Stravinsky was asked if one must be a believer to compose in the forms related to the church. Characteristically Stravinsky answered with directness, "Certainly, and not merely a believer in 'symbolic figures,' but in the Person of the Lord, the Person of the Devil, and the miracles of the church." He added, "Religious music without religion is almost always vulgar."

Stravinsky had a genuine humility before God. It is not surprising to learn that he began his day with prayer. He recognized that the "principal virtue of music is a means of communication with God." "The Church knew what the Psalmist knew: Music praises God," Stravinsky commented in *Conversations*. "Music is as well or better able to praise Him than the building of the church and all its decoration; it is the Church's greatest ornament. . . . The music of the 19th and 20th centuries—it is all secular—is 'expressively' and 'emotionally' beyond anything in the music of the earlier centuries; the 'angst' in *Lulu* . . . or tension in Schönberg's music. I say simply . . . that 'left to our own devices,' we are poor by many musical forms." Stravinsky started the "Back to Bach" movement and said that the heart of every musician's study should be the cantatas of Johann Sebastian Bach.

With still over 30 years of his life ahead of him, Stravinsky had to undergo many radical, difficult changes. In 1938 and 1939 his wife, daughter, and mother died, and because of the outbreak of World War II, he left Europe to go to the United States, even though he had become a French citizen in 1934.

After a year or so, he and his new wife, the painter Vera de Bosset, settled in Hollywood, and in 1945 Stravinsky became an American citizen. Over the years some critics and listeners became disconcerted by his various changes of style, but we need to remember that he was a man who lived in three worlds. With his lively mind he was always interested in what was going on around him. At no time was Stravinsky content to rest on his laurels. He was always eager to adventure in new directions and explore fresh musical territory. Ramuz in a letter to Stravinsky said, "What I perceived in you was an appetite and feeling for life, a love of all that is living; and that for you all that is living is potentially music."

By now, many of the idiosyncracies that proved upsetting at a first hearing of Stravinsky have fallen into proper perspective. Nadia Boulanger spoke of the wonderful continuity that underlined the whole of Stravinsky's work.

In 1951 Stravinsky conducted the first performance of his opera, *The Rake's Progress,* with words by W. H. Auden, at the Theater La Fenice in Venice, one of his favorite cities. It is his only full opera and is in the style of Mozart. While working on this score, he invited Robert Craft, a young American musician, to assist him. It was successful, and soon afterwards Craft became his musical assistant.

Craft's liking for the serial technique influenced Stravinsky to study the works of Schönberg, Berg, and Webern. Gradually he introduced the 12-tone row into his last works, such as the *Requiem Canticles.* These works are much briefer than his tonal compositions, but they still sound like Stravinsky. Even the serial technique went through the Stravinsky filter. These pieces make up only a small part of his total work. Stravinsky had an amazing ability to change and renew his musical thought. He never believed in using a formula. Each of his compositions has a different instrumental specification and a different sound. One can always expect the unusual in Stravinsky.

In Stravinsky's music there is no padding. He did all his composing at the piano, and he must have listened over and over to what he was writing to purge out unnecessary notes. Stravinsky was probably the first completely successful anti-Wagnerian in that he discarded the entire Wagnerian apparatus in favor, first of Russian Nationalism, then Neo-classicism, and last his American Period. His was a complete rupture with Romanticism. Stravinsky had a certain tidiness which characterized his intellect, his work habits, and his way of life. He had his *small* idiosyncracies though, as his wife, Vera, enjoyed writing about in a letter to a cousin in Moscow: "Igor's day is carefully routined. It begins with a headache which, however, is dispelled or forgotten in the shower. His bathroom, incidentally, looks like a prescription department in a pharmacy. . . . The vials of medicines, all neatly labeled in Russian by Igor himself, may be counted to the hundreds, and that, as the Americans say, is an underexaggeration. A branch-office drug store has gone into business on his night table . . . they are so mixed up with the sacred medals that I fear he will swallow a Saint Christopher some night instead of a sleeping pill. Igor once told me that he acquired his taste for medicines at the precocious age of five. . . . It follows that he is also concerned with the health of people near him. Puff your cheeks in his presence and very likely he will give you a carminative: or cough . . . and instantly one of his silver pillboxes will appear and you will be obliged to swallow a grain of anti-plague or other sugar-coated placebo—as I suppose them to be." (Craft, *Conversations*).

Because Stravinsky had a long, productive life, obviously, I have been able to mention only some of his compositions, but there is still one I want to call to your attention, and that is *Threni*. It was his first work to be conceived exclusively in the 12-tone technique. It is a work of enormous dignity and restraint. He wrote it in 1958, and the words are taken from the Lamentations of the Prophet Jeremiah. In *Threni*, according to Machlis, we see that Stravinsky's "personal belief in man's need to submit to God works hand in hand with his equally strong belief in the artist's need to submit to order and discipline. Given this conception of art, it should have come as no surprise that Stravinsky ended by submitting to the most severe musical discipline our age has yet devised."

Although Picasso was an atheist and Stravinsky a person who respected God, nevertheless, one finds certain parallels between these two artistic friends who knew each other from the ballet days in Paris. Each was a brilliant craftsman. Both of them used distortion for expressive purposes, and in their long lives they had various stylistic periods.

Ill health caused Stravinsky to slow down in his last years, though as late as 1970 he was working on instrumental transcriptions of some of Bach's preludes and fugues. Igor Stravinsky died in 1971 in New York City and was buried next to Diaghilev on the Island of San Michele near Venice, at his request. His extraordinary personality lives on through his music and the many books written about him.

Recommended Reading

Austin, William W. *Music in the 20th Century From Debussy Through Stravinsky*. New York: W. W. Norton, 1966.

Stravinsky, Igor and Craft, Robert. *Conversations with Igor Stravinsky*. London: Faber and Faber, 1958.

White, Eric Walter. *Stravinsky: A Critical Survey.* New York: Philosophical Library, 1948.

Recommended Listening

Apollo
Le Baiser de la Fée (The Fairy Kiss)
Firebird Suite
L'Histoire du Soldat (The Soldier's Tale)
Orpheus
Petrouchka
Pulcinella
Renard (Fox)
Le Sacre du Printemps (The Rite of Spring)
Song of the Nightingale
Symphony of Psalms
Threni

Chapter XX

Francis Poulenc
(1899-1963)

"I have sought neither to ridicule nor to mimic tradition, but to compose naturally as I felt impelled to."—Poulenc

Francis Poulenc and Arnold Schönberg were as different as Winnie the Pooh and Eyeore in their outlook on life and in their creativity. Shortly after World War I, Poulenc and his friend, Milhaud, were invited to visit Schönberg at his home in Mödling on the outskirts of Vienna. Poulenc, who was not a philosopher, went along reluctantly. Austria was still suffering from poverty and inflation. There was an air of depression everywhere, although the Schönberg house and garden were well kept. Inside, however, was worse than outside as the walls of the various rooms were lined with Schönberg's expressionistic paintings, mostly facial studies in which only the eyes were visible (reminiscent of Kokoschka's influence).

As soon as the formal greetings were extended, the conversation became incomprehensible to Poulenc, who listened without comment as Schönberg and Milhaud gravely discussed abstract philosophy and the 12-tone row. Poulenc found it doubly hard to concentrate with all the eyes peering at him from the portraits on the walls, and he kept glancing out of the open window at a small boy playing in the garden. Suddenly, the child lost control of the ball he was bouncing, and as if it were "on target," the missile flew through the window and landed in the center of the soup tureen, spraying a thick brown liquid over the table and all those around it. As Harding says, "The diversion was not unwelcome to Poulenc. His interest in Schönberg, genuine though it was, can be explained by the attraction of opposites."

Francis Poulenc, the Parisian musician par excellence, was born in Paris not far from the Presidential Palace of the Elysée. His father, a successful businessman, was part owner of a drug company. His mother, a thoroughgoing Parisian, was interested in the arts, especially the theater. She played the piano well and gave Poulenc his first lessons when he was five. He loved hearing his mother play Mozart, Chopin, Schubert, Schumann, and Grieg, all of whom influenced his music. Schubert's *Winter Journey* songs made a lasting impression on him.

Poulenc was a rather sickly child, born after his parents had been married many years. He was the delight of the household, and even as a man, Poulenc was like a charming, overgrown schoolboy. Early in life he decided to be a composer. His father saw to the completion of his academic education first, but allowed the piano lessons to continue. At an early age Poulenc was dictating compositions to his mother.

As soon as Poulenc's mother had taught him all she knew, she put him in the hands of various teachers, the most important one being the Spanish pianist, Ricardo Viñes who was an outstanding interpreter of Debussy, Ravel, de Falla, and Satie. Viñes not only introduced the 15-year-old Poulenc to as much music as possible, especially contemporary music, but he also introduced him to Erik Satie, and to another one of his pupils, George Auric. After Poulenc became famous, he said of Viñes, "I owe him everything." Poulenc became a brilliant pianist although his own solo piano music is somewhat too facile. His splendid Concerto in D Minor for 2 Pianos, showing the influence of Mozart, still has the unique and beautiful Poulenc sound. Poulenc and Auric became lifelong friends. He was awed by Auric's musical knowledge, brilliance, and sophistication, and inspired to work harder himself. The friends played through stacks of music that covered Auric's piano, went to concerts, and made friends with other musicians and artists they met in cafés.

A number of young composers were encouraged by Erik Satie and Jean Cocteau to give concerts in a Montparnasse studio. Six of these musicians, Francis Poulenc, George Auric, Darius Milhaud, Arthur Honegger, Germaine Tailleferre, and Louis Durey became known as "Les Six." The name came into being through the critic, Henri Collet, writing about a concert given by them. "Les Six," bound only by personal friendship and a desire to stand against Wagner and the German influence, as well as Impressionism, had little in common other than their youthfulness, high spirits, and the desire to further their compositions. Musically they had no unifying aesthetic.

Poulenc was the youngest of "Les Six," and his piece, *Rapsodie Nègre* (Negro Rhapsody) launched "Les Six," as well as himself. The composition made an impression at its first playing, because of the color, spice, and vigor of Poulenc's style. It had a melodic freshness all his own. He was only 18.

Before we go on with Poulenc, mention must be made of Erik Satie (1866-1925) who influenced many of the French composers. He had his eccentricities and weaknesses, but laziness was not one of them. He was a tremendous worker, "much more ant than butterfly," said

Jean Cocteau. "Satie teaches what in our age, is the greatest audacity—simplicity." His ballet *Parade* (about a circus), written for Diaghilev, with scenario by Cocteau and sets by Picasso, had a profound impact on modern theater. On one concert platform Satie appeared in a fireman's shining brass helmet so he would not go unnoticed. He has been called the "Father of humor in modern music." One of his many quotes is, "I want to compose a piece for dogs, and I already have my decor. The curtain rises on a bone." He was a rebel, but not in an angry way.

His insistence on extreme brevity, clarity, and simplicity had a great influence on his friend, Debussy, on Stravinsky, and later on the early compositions of Poulenc. Twentieth-century music owes much to Erik Satie. Simply expressed, his goal was to create an "everyday music" for everyday people—music that is down-to-earth, stripped of pretentions and ivory-tower seclusion. "All great artists are amateurs," said Satie. One of "Les Six," Milhaud, in speaking of Erik Satie, said, "The purity of his art, his horror of all concessions, his contempt for money, and his ruthless attitude toward the critics were a marvelous example for us all."

In 1918 Poulenc was called to military service in France. This interrupted his musical career, though he did write three exquisite piano pieces, *Mouvements perpetuels*. These are melodic, cheerful, Parisian two-part inventions of vivid charm without development or complication. Already one is aware of the importance of rhythm and jazz in Poulenc's music. After his release from military duties, he returned to composition with even greater zest.

In 1919 Poulenc composed his first songs to the poems of Guillaume Apollinaire. *Le Bestiaire* (Bestiary), with woodcuts by Raoul Dufy, is now a much sought after rare book edition. Poulenc is a musical counterpart to the painter Dufy. Raoul Dufy (1877-1953), best known for his lively decorative paintings, used bright, cheerful colors and a simple style to portray the world as he saw it. He was an artist who never really lost his enjoyment and appreciation of life, even after he became badly crippled with arthritis. Someone said that Dufy always looked like "an amazed cherub." He captured sensations in all their freshness and immediacy. He painted a happy world. He too loved music and painted individual instruments as well as entire orchestras.

Even though Poulenc already had a reputation as an able composer, he felt he did not really know how to write music correctly. So at the age of 21 he went to an excellent teacher, Charles Koechlin, to study harmony. His weekly exercises consisted of chorales in the form of four part harmonizations on themes of Bach. He worked hard for three years, and this was the whole of his formal education in the theory of music. As Hughes says, "Poulenc probably composed more from instinct and aural experience than any major composer of this century." He had a deeply musical temperament.

Once Poulenc tried to write a string quartet. Unsatisfied, he threw it in a Paris sewer. Basically he wrote compositions in small forms. He never wrote a symphony, but some of his chamber works, such as the Sonata for Oboe and the Sonata for Flute are filled with beautiful melodies. His woodwind music, for which the French are famous, is polished and witty. Poulenc learned orchestration mainly from listening to recordings and then examining the scores meticulously to learn how to get the sounds he liked.

Among the many artistic people Poulenc knew in Paris was Igor Stravinsky. It was Stravinsky who suggested to Diaghilev that "Poulenc might be able to compose a good ballet." *Les Biches (The House Party)* was given its première in Paris in 1924. For this, his first big work, Poulenc wrote the scenario as well as the score, and it was a success. The sets and costumes were by Marie Laurencin and the choreographer was Nijinska, Nijinsky's sister.

Poulenc was well into his 30's before he began to write his finest songs. Today he is known as the greatest exponent of the art song in the 20th century. His more than 130 songs include several song cycles. The dominant element in his music is melody, and his songs often begin immediately with the voice. He began to write more sensitively and powerfully after he started to accompany Pierre Bernac in song recitals. In my student days at Juilliard Music School we often went to concerts at Town Hall in New York City. A memorable evening was a concert given by Francis Poulenc and Pierre Bernac. Afterwards my friends and I went up to thank these wonderful artists for their music. In my excitement, after I had expressed my appreciation, not knowing what else to say, I asked Poulenc how to pronounce his name. With an amused smile he answered, "It rhymes with bank."

Poulenc had a keen ear for poetry, and he ranks with Bizet and Debussy, both of whom are known for the excellence of their settings of French to music. Poulenc had a vast literary and artistic culture and curiosity. Some of his favorite poets were Apollinaire, Éluard, and Max Jacob.

His *Concert champêtre* (Rustic Concerto, 1928) for harpsichord and orchestra, composed for the great harpsichordist, Wanda Landowska, with an emphasis on rhythm, was written to show that the harpsichord is not an archaic instrument. This music is filled with laughter and sunshine which we invariably associate with Poulenc.

Poulenc's nature had contrasting sides—the lighthearted and the sacred, the rebel and the conservative, the boisterous and melancholic. In the 1930's two incidents occurred which had a profound effect on him and caused him to think more deeply about life and death. For the first time Poulenc had financial problems, and then in the middle 1930's his deeply religious nature was awakened by the tragic death of his close friend, Ferroud, in an automobile accident. Soon after he began composing religious works, and with his wonderful compassion and humanity they are, according to Ewen, "some of his noblest and most spiritual writing."

To understand Poulenc, we must realize that he placed great value on being regarded as lighthearted, charming, sophisticated, even frivolous. His friends were always happy when he walked into a cafè, because they knew he would make them laugh, but behind his spontaneity and cheerfulness was hidden inner turmoil. As a friend observed, "Poulenc has two faces. One is smiling, the other serious." Poulenc, not one to speak about his private life, on a rare occasion described himself as "a melancholic character who likes to laugh like all melancholic characters." For years he was considered the clown of "Les Six," but his later years and music took on a more serious vein.

After turning back to his Roman Catholic faith in 1936, Poulenc began writing a series of religious works. He is considered one of the major composers of liturgical music in the 20th century. In 1937 he wrote the Mass in G for unaccompanied mixed choir, dedicated to his father. There was little church music of consequence being written in France at the time, and Poulenc brought the needed astringent touch which helped revive liturgical music. His choral works show his greatest originality and richness of thought.

Poulenc brought a remarkable and telling simplicity to church music which in France seemed imprisoned until released by Poulenc's lightness of touch, satire, and wit. The majority of his choral works are for a capella choirs. Poulenc is one of the few modern French composers to reintroduce an authentic religious note into French music. In all of Poulenc's religious compositions there is a mingled sweetness and humility, a tenderness and simplicity of heart that causes the music to remain in the memory. A conservative, Poulenc never lost contact with the past. He had something to say and he said it with style and personality from his heart. He pursued a lifelong study of Bach.

Poulenc spent the war years, 1940-1945, mostly in Paris. In 1943 he composed music to Louis Aragon's haunting reflection on the Nazi occupation of France. Entitled simply "C," it is one of the most magnificent of his songs.

Some of Poulenc's most delightful music is found in his setting of the children's story, *Babar, the Elephant.* His *Les Animaux modeles,* a ballet based on the fables of La Fontaine is rich in harmony and orchestration.

Between 1953 and 1956 Poulenc worked on the music for *Dialogues des Carmelites* (Dialogues of the Carmelites). The text was taken from the superb play by George Bernanos. Poulenc followed the words with great care. His intention was to make the words heard: the voice is of prime importance, never the orchestra. It is an intensely emotional work.

One very snowy day in the Swiss Alps we built a fire in the fireplace, found both the music and the words and listened to a recording of the *Dialogues* from beginning to end. It made a lasting impression and reminded us how often we only half-listen to music. To heighten one's appreciation of music it is helpful to follow the score and listen carefully to the words, when there are words.

The story is about a group of Carmelite nuns who refused to disband during the French Revolution and suffered martyrdom. The main theme is the psychology of fear. While composing the opera, Poulenc had a nervous breakdown. He spent several weeks in a clinic wrestling with the terrible twins, self-doubt and fear of death. He was unable to work for months. Poulenc, like his heroine, Blanche, lived in fear of everything and of nothing, of liberty and constraint. The final scene of martyrdom, as the nuns mount the guillotine, is unforgettable. At the last, Blanche has victory over fear as she goes to her death trusting in the Triune God of the universe. One feels it is Poulenc's victory too.

Poulenc, as many great artists, borrowed countless melodic ideas from such composers as Mozart, Chopin, Franck, Tchaikovsky, Mussorgsky, Chabrier and Puccini. It was not that he had no ideas himself, but because of his love for the music of these composers he made their music become a part of him. The music of Poulenc is as personal as any composed in this century. He had a gift of improvisation and a free melodic abundance, yet he worked very hard at composition, always composing at the piano. Milhaud spoke of "the fresh charm of Poulenc's music." Music was melody to Poulenc. His clear, simple art renewed the wonderful tradition of Scarlatti and Mozart.

One of Poulenc's most scintillating works is *Gloria.* It is a joyful, radiant piece of music. Poulenc is as much as anybody in this age "a merry man of God in his music," and he received the same reproaches that were made about Haydn and his high spirited religious music. Poulenc undoubtedly responded much the same—that the thought of God made him happy. *Gloria,* written in 1959, is in the style of Vivaldi. It is in six sections, with each part very much a contrast to the next. It is a sincere composition, deeply felt and filled with sunshine.

Poulenc never married. Like Schubert, friendship was everything to him, and he had a large circle of friends. He loved Paris, but he also enjoyed his home, garden and flowers outside the city. He was a connoisseur of painting, poetry, food, and wine. He owned several small works by Braque, Dufy, Marie Laurencin, Matisse, and Picasso.

Poulenc died suddenly of heart failure on January 30, 1963. His date book, which ordinarily was filled with many future appointments, had no entry beyond the day on which he died, and he left behind no unfinished compositions. As Erik Routley says, "Francis Poulenc's death in 1963 was one of those events which made one feel that a light had gone out." Poulenc was not the universal composer in the sense that Beethoven and Mozart were, but he sang his song, and it was beautiful.

Recommended Reading

Hardling, James. *The Ox on the Roof.* New York: St. Martin's Press, 1972.

Hell, Henri. *Francis Poulenc.* London: John Calder, 1959.

Meyers, Rollo. *Erik Satie.* New York: Dover Publications, 1968.

Recommended Listening

Animaux Modèles
Concert champêtre
Concerto in G Minor for Organ and Orchestra
Concerto for Two Pianos and Orchestra
Dialogues of the Carmelites
Gloria
Mass in G
Mouvements Perpétuels
Sonata for Flute and Piano
Sonata for Oboe and Piano
Songs: "Le Bestiaire," "Tel Jour," "Telle Nuit," "Sanglots"
Story of Babar, The Elephant
Satie: *Parade*

Postlude

In order not "to walk into the future backwards," we must be careful not to shut ourselves off from the culture around us, and particularly, the developments in 20th-century music. Those of us at L'Abri Fellowship are deeply interested in saving the good in culture and warmly affirm the following statement by J. G. Machen: "The Christian cannot be satisfied as long as any human activity is either opposed to Christianity or out of all connection with Christianity. . . . The Christian, therefore, cannot be indifferent to any branch of earnest human endeavor. It must all be brought into some relation to the gospel."*

We have seen clearly in these chapters that God has given incredible gifts to His created men and women and the liberty to use them. We have also seen that there are different points of departure. Bach chose to draw on the Scriptures, "the well of life," for his inspiration and creativity. A contemporary of Bach, Andreas Werckmeister, spoke of music as "a gift of God to be used only in His honor."

*J. G. Machen, *Christianity and Culture* (Huémoz, Switzerland: L'Abri Fellowship, 1969) p. 4.

Less than one hundred years later, as the influence of the Enlightenment with its rejection of biblical Christianity began to be felt, Dr. Charles Burney in his *General History of Music* wrote that music is an innocent luxury, unnecessary, indeed, to our existence, but a great improvement and gratification of the sense of hearing.

Now that we are near the end of the 20th century, humanism, leading to despair, has taken over much of music. "My religion needs no God, only faith," said the philosophically-orientated Schönberg, and he placed great emphasis on expressing oneself. As individuals turn further and further from the personal, infinite God, the Giver of gifts, the more dehumanized and twisted will be that which he or she creates. We have already arrived at the computer age of man thinking himself a machine listening to a machine.

We are not speaking of something unimportant, although some may feel that art, music, and literature are the extras in life. Alfred Einstein in his book, *Greatness in Music,* made this startling statement: "Artistic greatness is both more permanent and universal than historical greatness." Remembering that the Christian Church from the first made use of the arts, we should be challenged to have them take their proper place again. As Martin Luther said, "I feel strongly that all the arts, and particularly music, should be placed in the service of Him who has created and given them." The arts in a Christian framework are an act of worship, and we should be willing to work on them, striving to make artistic statements worthy of the Lord in whom we believe.

There are no simple answers. We may have raised more questions than we have been able to answer. We are not against change and modern techniques, although some will weaken and some strengthen the content. The marvelous message of Christianity should not be presented in an old-fashioned way. There is the lostness of man, but ultimately, the Christian should be hopeful and not write music that is harmful in this fallen world. We are called to make a personal contribution either as producers or appreciators of art.

We hope there will be those who are encouraged to struggle and find solutions, so that increasingly the great gift of music will be used for the glory of God.

—Jane Stuart Smith

Appendix

Music in the Flow of History and the Arts

	PERIOD	MUSIC	ARTS
ANCIENT HISTORY	4500—1100 B.C. Egypt Assyria Babylon Persia	Biblical Psalms	Pyramids Palace of Sargon II Ishtar Gate Persepolis
CLASSIC	1100 B.C.—500 A.D. (Crucifixion of Christ c. 33 A.D.) Greek Roman—Etruscan	History of Western Music Begins c. 200 A.D. 8 Modes	Acropolis Pompei
MEDIEVAL	500—1400 A.D. Byzantine Romanesque Gothic	Gregorian Chant Polyphony Ars Antique Ars Nova	Mosaics Cathedral Pisa Cathedral Chartres Dante
RENAISSANCE	1450—1600 Quattrocento Cinquecento Reformation 1517 Counter-Reformation	Ockeghem Josquin Des Prés Luther Chorales—Genevan Psalter Palestrina	Giotto Da Vinci, Raphael, Michelangelo Dürer Cranach Rubens

Era	Period / Style	Music	Art / Literature
BA-ROQUE	1600—1750 Early Baroque High Baroque	Schütz Vivaldi, Bach, Handel	Rembrandt Milton
NEO-CLASSIC	18th CENTURY (Age of Reason)	Haydn, Mozart Beethoven, Schubert	David Schwind Goethe
ROMANTIC	19th CENTURY 1st Half: Romanticism 2nd Half: Nationalism Post-Romanticism Impressionism	Mendelssohn, Lizt, Chopin, Wagner, Verdi, Brahms Tchaikovsky, Dvorak Mahler Debussy, Ravel, Delius	Delacroix Repin Van Gogh Monet, Cezanne, Sisley
AGE OF SCIENCE	20th CENTURY Expressionism Abstract Many Styles Non-Objective	Schönberg (Atonality, (12-tone Row) Berg, Webern Bartok Satie, Stravinsky (Jazz) Poulenc Electronic Music (Machine) Stockhausen, Cage (Chance)	Kandinsky, Kokoschka Munch T. S. Eliot Gris, Braque Picasso Dufy, Matisse Duchamp Pollock

Select Bibliography

Apel, Willi. *Harvard Dictionary of Music.* Cambridge, Mass.: Harvard University Press, 1969.

Bukofzer, Manfred F. *Music in the Baroque Era.* New York: W. W. Norton, 1947.

Burney, Charles. *A General History of Music.* London: G. T. Foulis and Co., 1935.

Chase, Gilbert. *The Music of Spain.* New York: Dover Publications, 1959.

Durant, Will. *The Story of Philosophy.* New York: Simon and Schuster, 1953.

Einstein, Alfred. *Music in the Romantic Era.* New York: W. W. Norton, 1947.

Ewen, D. *Ewen's Musical Masterworks: The Encyclopedia of Musical Masterpieces.* New York: Bonanza Books, 1949.

Grout, Donald Jay. *A History of Western Music.* New York: W. W. Norton, 1960.

Grove, George. *Dictionary of Music and Musicians.* New York: The MacMillan Co., 1928.

Julian, John. *A Dictionary of Hymnology.* New York: Dover Publications, 1957.

Lang, Paul Henry. *Music in Western Civilization.* New York: W. W. Norton, 1941.

——————, and Bettmann, Otto. *A Pictorial History of Music.* New York: W. W. Norton, 1960.

——————, and Broder, Nathan (eds.). *Contemporary Music in Europe. A Comprehensive Survey.* New York: G. Schirmer, 1965.

Leonard, Richard Anthony. *A History of Russian Music.* New York: Minerva Press, 1956.

Lloyd, Norman. *The Golden Encyclopedia of Music.* New York: Golden Press, 1968.

Machlis, Joseph. *Introduction to Contemporary Music.* New York: The Golden Press, 1968.

246

_____. *The Enjoyment of Music.* New York: W. W. Norton, 1963.

Reese, Gustav. *Music in the Renaissance.* New York: W. W. Norton, 1959.

Schaeffer, Francis A. *How Should We Then Live.* Old Tappan, New Jersey: Fleming H. Revell, 1976.

Scholes, Percy A. *The Oxford Companion to Music.* London: Oxford University Press, 1974.

Schonberg, Harold C. *The Lives of the Great Composers.* New York: W. W. Norton, 1970.

Glossary

Anthem. A short choral work usually based on Scripture and performed in some Protestant churches by a chorus and soloists.

Antiphonal singing. Two soloists or groups alternating the singing of a religious text—as a Psalm.

Atonality. A contemporary practice in which no principle of key is observed.

Ballet. A theatrical art form using dancing to convey a story theme or atmosphere.

Baroque. German and Austrian music of the 17th and 18th centuries marked by improvisation, contrasting effects and powerful tensions.

Cantata. A work for several solo voices and a chorus much like a short oratorio or an opera, but without acting.

Canticle. A liturgical song taken from the Bible.

Chant. A simple harmonized melody used in some churches for singing unmetrical texts, principally the Psalms or canticles.

Chorale. A hymn or psalm sung to a traditional or composed melody in church.

Classical music. Music of a more formal nature with emphasis on beauty and proportion rather than on emotional expression.

Concerto. A piece for one or more soloists and orchestra usually in symphonic form with three contrasting movements.

Concerto grosso. A Baroque orchestral composition with a small group of solo instruments contrasting with the full orchestra.

Counterpoint. A part or voice added to another. Combination of parts or voices each significant in itself, resulting in a coherent texture.

Dissonance. An unresolved musical note or chord.

Enlightenment, The. A philosophic movement of the 18th century marked by questioning of traditional doctrines and

248

values, with a tendency toward individualism and an emphasis on the idea of universal human progress.

Folk Song. A song which has grown up among the peasantry of any race, transmitted orally from generation to generation, and usually sung without accompaniment.

Libretto. The text of an opera or oratorio.

Lied. A type of solo vocal composition that came into being as an outcome of the Romantic movement. The poem chosen is of high importance and not a mere passenger for the tune.

Modulation. Change of key in the course of a passage.

Opera. Drama set to music.

Oratorio. A music composition using soloists, chorus and orchestra. The subjects generally are taken from the Bible. There is no acting and scenery is not used.

Orchestration. The act of scoring for an orchestra.

Overture. Intrumental music intended as the inroduction to an opera or an oratorio.

Psalm. A hymn accompanied by stringed instruments. The Book of Psalms is the oldest book of songs still in use.

Reformation, The. A 16th century religious movement marked by rejection or modification of much of Roman Catholic doctrine and practice and the establishment of Protestant churches.

Romanticism. A literary, artistic and philosophical movement originating in the 18th century characterized by reaction against neoclassicism and emphasis on imagination and emotions with a predilection for melancholy.

Score. The copy of a musical composition in written or printed notation.

Serenade. A work for chamber orchestra, resembling a suite.

Sonata. An extended composition in several movements for one or two instruments.

Symphony. A usually long and complex sonata for orchestra.

Tonality. Loyalty to the key-scheme of a composition.

Twelve-tone row (or serial technique). A composing procedure employing the dodecaphonic scale in which the 12 notes are considered to be all of equal status.

Index